Following God

Paul's
Co-workers

Paul's Co-workers

A BIBLE STUDY BY

RICHARD SOULE

AMG *Publishers*.

Chattanooga, TN 37422

PAUL'S CO-WORKERS

Copyright © 2010 by Richard Soule
First Printing, April 2010

Published by AMG Publishers.

ISBN 13: 978-0-89957-342-7
ISBN 10: 0-89957-342-8

Cover design Michael Largent at Indoor Graphics, Chattanooga, TN
Text editing and page layout by Rick Steele and Jennifer Ross

Printed in Canada
14 13 12 11 10 –T– 6 5 4 3 2 1

Other new releases in the Following God® Series:

Life Principles for Spiritual Warfare

by Eddie Rasnake

and

Life Principles for Worship
from the Feasts of Israel

by Rick Shepherd

Look for these new Following God® study books in
your local Christian book stores or on our websites:
www.AMGPublishers.com
www.FollowingGod.com

About the Author

Richard M. "Dick" Soule was born in 1949 in Riverside, California. Both his father and his maternal grandfather were Navy doctors. Not surprisingly, he spent a couple of years in the Navy himself, but has spent most of his career in education-related activities. Dick is a graduate of Dartmouth College, obtained his Master's Degree at the University of New Hampshire, and completed doctoral coursework at Utah State University. Dick's spiritual journey has included stops in nearly as many places as his travels, but a loving brother and sister in Atlanta introduced him and his wife to the pure gospel in 1986. Dick currently serves as deacon for the Adult Teaching Ministry at Newark Church of Christ in Newark, Delaware, and lives with his wife in a moneypit house nearby.

About the Following God Series

Three authors and fellow ministers, Wayne Barber, Eddie Rasnake, and Rick Shepherd, teamed up in 1998 to write a character-based Bible study for AMG Publishers. Their collaboration developed into the title, *Life Principles from the Old Testament*. Since 1998 these same authors and AMG Publishers have produced five more character-based studies—each consisting of twelve lessons geared around a five-day study of a particular Bible personality. More studies of this type are in the works. In 2001, AMG Publishers launched a different Following God category called the Following God® Discipleship Series. The titles introduced in the Discipleship Series are among the first Following God® studies to be published in a topically-based format (rather than Bible character-based). However, the interactive study format that readers have come to love remains constant with each new Following God® release. As new titles and categories are being planned, our focus remains the same: to provide excellent Bible study materials that point people to God's Word in ways that allow them to apply truths to their own lives. More information on this groundbreaking series can be found on the following web pages:

www.AMGPublishers.com

www.FollowingGod.com

Preface

We all need heroes. Some of us choose political heroes; others, sports or entertainment. It is not very fashionable these days to have biblical heroes, but both Old and New Testaments are replete with people whose courage, faith, and commitment serve as better models—despite or sometimes because of their flaws—than anyone we're likely to find in modern culture. Perhaps we don't choose biblical heroes because the primary characters—Moses, Abraham, Deborah, Ruth, David, Peter, Mary, Paul, or John—seem larger than life to us, people we could never hope to match.

The apostle Paul has been a particular interest of mine for some years—not so much Paul himself, although he is complex and fascinating, but rather the people who worked with him. In many cases, they faced the same daunting challenges he did and like him emerged victorious. This study focuses on a particular group of Paul's associations, those he named as co-workers. The Greek word for these friends of Paul is *sunergos*, a combination of *sun* (with) and *ergon* (labor); to denote a co-worker—one who labors alongside another—Paul uses the phrase *sunergos sunergos*.

Paul's letters name fifteen co-workers, provided in the list that follows in the order Paul cites them. The starred co-workers are the subjects of the chapters in this study.

*Prisca (Priscilla) and her husband, Aquila (Romans 16:3)
Urbanus (Romans 16:9)
Timothy (Romans 16:21; 1 Thessalonians 3:2)
*Titus (2 Corinthians 8:23)
*Epaphroditus (Philippians 2:25)
Clement (Philippians 4:3)
*Euodia and Syntyche (Philippians 4:2–3)
*Aristarchus (Colossians 4:10–11; Philemon 1:24)
*John Mark (Colossians 4:10–11; Philemon 1:24)
Jesus Justus (Colossians 4:11)
*Philemon (Philemon 1:1)
Luke (Philemon 1:24)
*Demas (Philemon 1:24)

With the exception of Timothy, John Mark, and Luke, these are not exactly people who get a lot of ink in the New Testament, which is one of the compelling things about them. These are ordinary people thrust into extraordinary events. Prisca and Aquila, Epaphroditus, and Aristarchus genuinely risked their lives. Euodia and Syntyche, Demas, and John Mark displayed their shortcomings.

Whether you picked up this study looking for heroes, hoping for more understanding of the New Testament, or just out of curiosity, I think you'll find the stories of these people interesting and challenging. After working your way through it, I hope you'll find yourself closer to God and motivated to find additional ways you can serve Him.

In Him,
Dick Soule

Special Note: Because several of Paul's co-workers are connected with the books of Colossians, Philemon, and/or Philippians, three of Paul's prison epistles, the date and location of the writing affect the interpretation of their lives. Traditionally, these letters have all been ascribed to Paul's first Roman imprisonment in AD 60–62, but other scholars suggest Paul may have written them from Ephesus. I mention this several times in these studies, and sometimes I use the Rome scenario; other times, the Ephesus scenario. Ultimately, it doesn't matter, and you can accept either tradition.

This work is dedicated to its subjects—the many unknown Christians who labor to spread the message of Christ Jesus in an unbelieving world. In the first century, they were primarily responsible for the unlikely spread of Christianity in the Roman Empire. Today, they continue that work at home and abroad.

Table of Contents

1

Prisca and Aquila
Courage and Commitment

Of all Paul's co-workers, Scripture tells us the most about Prisca and Aquila (although the information must be pieced together from six different citations in Acts, Romans, 1 Corinthians, and 2 Timothy). They are the only married couple mentioned prominently in the New Testament, and their extensive movement across the Mediterranean world testifies to their unequivocal commitment to Paul's missions and the spread of the gospel.

In a parenthetical remark in his *Lives of the Caesars*, written in about AD 110, the Roman historian Suetonius reported that Emperor Claudius expelled some Jews from Rome in about AD 49 because of "disturbances at the instigation of Chrestus" [probably a misspelling of *Christus*]. Conflicts between Jews and Christians were not uncommon in the earliest days of the church, particularly since Christianity was, at that point, considered a sect of Judaism by Roman authorities. Mainstream Jews viewed the beliefs of the Jesus followers about His divinity as blasphemous. Aquila and Prisca were among the Jews who left Rome.

Why they went to Corinth instead of a closer town within Italy is uncertain, but it may have been a business decision based on good economic opportunities in Corinth. The city had been destroyed by the Roman general Lucius Mummius in 146 BC after a series of perceived insults to Rome by Corinthians, but it was reestablished in 44 BC by Julius Caesar and colonized primarily by freed

Put Yourself In Their Shoes
PRISCA AND AQUILA

Prisca (*PRIS-ka*)—"ancient" or Priscilla—"little Prisca"

Aquila (*ak-OO-la*)—"eagle"

Prisca and Aquila were Jews from Rome. (Aquila's ancestors came from Pontus.) They first met Paul in Corinth in AD 51 or 52.

"Greet Prisca and Aquila, my fellow workers in Christ Jesus, who risked their necks for my life, to whom not only I give thanks but all the churches of the Gentiles give thanks as well. Greet also the church in their house." (Romans 16:3–5)

Did You Know?
CORINTH

The seaport city of Corinth, a key cross-road between Rome and the East, was both an economic boom town and a hotbed of immorality, comparable to American gold-rush cities in the nineteenth century or modern Las Vegas, with similar opportunities and challenges.

slaves. As one of the fastest-growing cities in the empire, located at the strategic crossroad between Rome and the East, Corinth was a real boom town.

On the other hand, Corinth also had a reputation as one of the most sordid cities in the empire. With a reported one thousand prostitutes serving at the temple of Diana (Aphrodite), Corinth became synonymous with fornication (*Korinthiaszomai*). According to the Greek geographer Strabo (about 63 BC–AD 24), "The temple of Aphrodite was so rich that it owned more than a thousand temple slaves, courtesans, whom both men and woman had dedicated to the goddess. And therefore it was on account of these women that the city was crowded with people and grew rich; for instance, the ship captains freely squandered their money, and hence the proverb, 'Not for every man is the voyage to Corinth.'" Such an atmosphere may have been attractive to enthusiastic Christians seeking to expand the influence of the gospel, so Prisca and Aquila's motivation may have been missional.

COMMITTED TO HOSPITALITY

Paul arrived in Corinth in about AD 51, during his second missionary journey. He had sent his close associates Silas and Timothy back to Thessalonica to strengthen the church there, while he went on to Athens, where he attempted to reason with the philosophers.

📖 Read Acts 17:16–34 and answer the questions that follow.

How did Paul approach sharing the gospel in Athens?

_____

_____

_____

_____

First, Paul went to the synagogues; then he preached in public places. He spent time trying to understand the city, using his observations as part of his lesson to the philosophers in the Areopagus.

Describe the response Paul received.

_____

_____

_____

In Athens, Paul seems to have received his least enthusiastic response. Perhaps Athenians were too used to hearing new things, as Luke wrote (Acts 17:21), and could not see how Paul's message differed substantially from dozens of other speakers.

Acts 17 ends rather abruptly with Paul leaving Athens even though some said they wanted to hear him again.

APPLY Why do you think Paul didn't stay in Athens longer?

_____

_____

We don't know what prompted Paul to move on before Timothy and Silas returned, but I suspect he was worn out, exasperated with the Athenians, and a bit lonely.

> *"After this Paul left Athens and went to Corinth. And he found a Jew named Aquila, a native of Pontus, recently come from Italy with his wife Priscilla, because Claudius had commanded all the Jews to leave Rome. And he went to see them, and because he was of the same trade he stayed with them and worked, for they were tentmakers by trade."* (Acts 18:1–3)

 APPLY What do you think Paul's mood may have been when he first arrived in Corinth? Why?

_____

_____

Paul may have been a bit discouraged when he arrived, anxious for Timothy and Silas to return from the north and disheartened by the relative unresponsiveness of the Athenians.

How did Prisca and Aquila immediately provide comfort for Paul?

_____

_____

Because Aquila and Prisca were fellow tentmakers, Paul probably enjoyed putting aside preaching temporarily and just working with his hands, something he valued (1 Thessalonians 4:11).

The hospitality practiced by Aquila and Prisca was not limited to their service to Paul—they also hosted house churches. Paul, writing to Corinth from Ephesus, adds their greetings to the church in Corinth (1 Corinthians 16:19). Later, just before his execution in Rome in about AD 66, he greets their house church in Ephesus (2 Timothy 4:19).

In the time of the New Testament, small groups of Christians met in private homes. In the very earliest days of the church, the apostles are said to have taught and preached *"from house to house"* (Acts 5:42). When Saul (later Paul) sought to persecute Christians, he sought them out in *"house after house"* (Acts 8:3). After his Damascus Road conversion, Paul also taught *"from house to house"* (Acts 20:20).

Besides Aquila and Prisca, we know of several other house-church hosts:
- Mary, the mother of John Mark in Jerusalem (Acts 12:12)
- Gauis in Corinth (Romans 16:23)
- Jason in Thessalonica (Acts 17:5)
- Philip in Caesarea (Acts 21:8)
- Nympha in Colossae (Colossians 4:15)
- Philemon in Colossae (Philemon 1:2)

WERE AQUILA AND PRISCA CHRISTIANS WHEN THEY FIRST MET PAUL?

Neither Luke (in Acts) nor Paul (in his letters) tell us whether Aquila and Prisca were Christians when they first encountered Paul, but it seems likely. Would Paul, who later wrote, *"Do not be unequally yoked with unbelievers"* (2 Corinthians 6:14) have both lived and worked with people who did not share his faith?

Acts 18:3 also seems to suggest that Paul may have already known of them before he arrived in Corinth.

Finally, if they had become Christians through Paul's ministry, it seems likely that Luke would have mentioned that.

A dissenting view holds that Christianity did not make its way to Rome until later, but Acts 2:10 tells us that there were *"visitors from Rome"* in Jerusalem on the day of Pentecost, when the Holy Spirit came upon Jesus' disciples.

 Word Study
CHURCH

The Greek word for church is *ekklesia*. Literally, according to *Strong's Exhaustive Concordance*, *ekklesia* means "a calling out." It was the term for assemblies of Greek citizens called to a meeting to discuss matters of importance.

In the New Testament, an *ekklesia* can be a small group meeting together, such as the Ephesian church meeting in the home of Aquila and Prisca (1 Corinthians 16:19), or the entire community of Christians in a city (see 1 Corinthians 1:2, for example), or the entire body of Christians throughout the world (see 1 Corinthians 12:28).

The church (*ekklesia*) is a group of people, called out by God, not a building.

New Testament Christians met in homes for a variety of reasons. First, in most communities, their numbers were small. Second, considering the persecution Christians faced in many towns, meeting in homes was safer. Third, there were no dedicated church buildings until at least the latter years of the second century.

APPLY Think about and respond to the following questions.

What would be involved in hosting a church in a home?

_____

_____

_____

_____

What are the advantages and disadvantages of small-group house churches versus large building-based churches?

_____

_____

_____

As Jews and noncitizens, Prisca and Aquila probably lived in the squalid apartment buildings (*insulae*) prevalent in every major Roman city. Their apartment would have been quite small, so hosting a house church represented a significant display of hospitality as well as their commitment to the church.

Prisca and Aquila

DAY TWO

COMMITTED TO MISSION

When Paul left Corinth after a stay of about eighteen months, Prisca and Aquila went with him:

"After this, Paul stayed many days longer and then took leave of the brothers and set sail for Syria, and with him Priscilla and Aquila. At Cenchreae he had cut his hair, for he was under a vow. And they came to Ephesus, and he left them there, but he himself went into the synagogue and reasoned with the Jews" (Acts 18:18–19).

Prisca and Aquila had left their home in Rome just four years earlier. Now they were moving to yet another unfamiliar city. What concerns would they have faced?

_____

_____

_____

Many of their concerns must have been much like those we might feel today—separating from church and other friends, acclimating to daily life in a new place, finding the best market, locating a new residence.

When Nero became emperor in AD 54, he lifted the ban on Jews in the imperial capital. Paul had a deep desire to bring the gospel to Rome (see Romans 1:15). He had never been there, but he knew two people who were native Romans.

If Paul asked Prisca and Aquila to return to Rome, what purpose could they have served?

_____

_____

_____

Prisca and Aquila could scout the Roman church landscape, discovering who the people were, where they met, and how they practiced.

Since Jewish Christians had not been in Rome for several years, what kinds of issues might Aquila and Prisca have uncovered in the Roman Gentile church?

_____

_____

_____

Even though there is a legend that Peter visited Rome, perhaps around AD 42, there is no hard evidence. It is possible the Roman church grew despite a lack of apostolic leadership. Consequently, there were almost certainly gaps and errors in their understanding of the gospel.

From 2 Timothy 4:19, we know that Prisca and Aquila were back in Ephesus by AD 66. They had four significant relocations in less than fifteen years (Rome to Corinth in about AD 49, Corinth to Ephesus in AD 53, Ephesus back to Rome in about AD 56, and Rome back to Ephesus before AD 66). Does such extensive travel in the ancient world surprise you?

What do these relocations tell you about the commitment Prisca and Aquila had to Paul's gospel?

_____

_____

_____

It should be obvious this couple were totally committed to helping Paul spread the gospel in any way they could.

Paul's heartfelt commendation of Prisca and Aquila in his letter to the church in Rome gives us the most compelling picture of this committed couple:

> *"Greet Prisca and Aquila, my fellow workers in Christ Jesus, who risked their necks for my life, to whom not only I give thanks, but all the churches of the Gentiles give thanks as well. Greet also the church in their house."* (Romans 16:3–5)

ROMANS 16

Some scholars believe the sixteenth chapter of Romans is not part of the original letter but rather a cover letter for a copy of Romans sent to Ephesus, and it is Paul's greeting to Prisca and Aquila (Romans 16:3) that is most frequently cited as evidence. They went to Ephesus in about AD 53–54 (Acts 18:18–19) and are again in Ephesus in about AD 66, when Paul greets them in his letter to Timothy (2 Timothy 4:19). Another piece of evidence is Paul's mention of Epaenetus, who is said to be *"the first convert in Asia"* (Romans 16:5).

Finally, Paul had never visited Rome when he wrote the letter, so some suggest he could not have known so many Roman Christians.

However, there is strong counter evidence. Paul also greeted the *"family of Aristobulus"* and one Herodion (Romans 16:10–11). These names strongly suggest household servants who had once served the Herodian family in Rome.

Paul's mission faced intense danger almost every place he visited, including each of the three cities in which Aquila and Prisca served.

- Corinthian Jews took him to court, accusing him of subversive teaching. (Read Acts 18:11–17 for an account of this incident).
- Irate artisans rioted when Paul's teaching cut into their trade—selling miniature reproductions of the temple of Artemis and statues of the goddess (Acts 19:23–41).
- Emperor Nero used Christians as scapegoats for the Great Fire of Rome in AD 64 as described by the Roman historian Tacitus in *Annals* (about AD 110). "Covered with the skins of beasts, they were torn by dogs and perished, or were nailed to crosses, or were doomed to the flames and burnt, to serve as a nightly illumination, when daylight had expired. Nero offered his gardens for the spectacle, and was exhibiting a show in the circus, while he mingled with the people in the dress of a charioteer or stood aloft on a car" (*Annals*, 15.44).
- According to tradition, Paul was beheaded in Rome near the end of the Neronian persecution.
- Prisca and Aquila traveled from Rome to Ephesus before or during Nero's persecution. Paul greets them in his final letter, 2 Timothy, which was probably written about AD 66. At that time, the church faced problems from another craftsman, Alexander (see 2 Timothy 4:14).

APPLY Why does the message of Christ Jesus threaten some people?

_____

_____

_____

There are probably dozens of reasons, but they all center on the need to respond to Jesus—once you hear about Him, your choice is to embrace Him or reject Him. Either can be frightening, and most of us respond to fear with anger.

As the church expanded in the second century, Roman leaders tried to kill the movement by hunting down and executing its leaders. Why did this tactic fail?

_____

_____

_____

Early Christianity, unlike today's version in many places, was not dominated by leaders. We read about Peter, Paul, and a few others, but Christianity was primarily a movement of ordinary people and was not dependent on leaders.

APPLY The second-century Christian writer Tertullian said that "the blood of martyrs is seed." What do you think he meant by this?

_____

_____

_____

COMMITTED TO SOUND TEACHING

Afewter just three weeks preaching in the synagogues of Ephesus, Paul departed for Syria, entrusting the immediate future of the church to Aquila and Prisca.

"Now a Jew named Apollos, a native of Alexandria, came to Ephesus. He was an eloquent man, competent in the Scriptures. He had been instructed in the way of the Lord. And being fervent in spirit, he spoke and taught accurately the things concerning Jesus, though he knew only the baptism of John. He began to speak boldly in the synagogue, but when Priscilla and Aquila heard him, they took him and explained to him the way of God more accurately. And when he wished to cross to Achaia, the brothers encouraged him and wrote to the disciples to welcome him. When he arrived, he greatly helped those who through grace had believed, for he powerfully refuted the Jews in public, showing by the Scriptures that the Christ was Jesus" (Acts 18:24–28).

What was lacking in Apollos' knowledge when he originally came to Ephesus?

_____

_____

Apollos did not know about Christian baptism, although he knew about baptism for repentance (that practiced by John the Baptist).

Why was it important to correct Apollos?

_____

_____

Christian baptism played a central role in the early church. As Paul explains (Romans 6:3–8), baptism is the mechanism through which the believer is united to Christ in a symbolic reenactment of the Savior's death and resurrection.

What approach did Aquila and Prisca take in teaching Apollos?

_____

_____

_____

By talking to him in private, they avoided the possibility of embarrassing Apollos in public and therefore damaging his effectiveness.

📖 Read 1 Corinthians 1:11–13; 3:2–9 and 16:12 (written from Ephesus).

The Corinthian congregation was threatened by factions claiming allegiance to different strong leaders (Peter, Paul, and Apollos). When Paul says he and Apollos are nothing, what is his point?

_____

_____

_____

Christianity is not about religious leaders; it's completely about Jesus Christ.

The confidence Paul placed in Prisca and Aquila is demonstrated by his having stationed them in Ephesus and perhaps sending them to Rome. How and why they returned later to Ephesus is not known. In AD 64, a terrible fire devastated much of Rome, and subsequent rumors blamed the blaze on Nero himself. To divert attention from these rumors, Nero made Christians scapegoats, subjecting them to torturous deaths. If Aquila and Prisca were still in Rome at this time, perhaps Paul urged them to flee back to Ephesus to assist the sometimes-timid Timothy (see 2 Timothy 1:6–7).

COMMITTED AS A COUPLE

A noteworthy fact about Prisca and Aquila is they are *always* mentioned together. They relocated together. They taught Apollos together. They hosted churches together. One is never mentioned without the other. They are the epitome of the Ephesians 5 marriage:

"Wives, submit to your own husbands, as to the Lord. For the husband is the head of the wife even as Christ is the head of the church, his body, and is himself its Savior. Now as the church submits to Christ, so also wives should submit in everything to their husbands. Husbands, love your wives, as Christ loved the church and gave himself up for her, that he might sanctify her, having cleansed her by the washing of water with the word, so that he might present the church to himself in splendor, without spot or wrinkle or any such thing, that she might be holy and without blemish. In the same way husbands should love their wives as their own bodies. He who loves his wife loves himself. For no one ever hated his own flesh, but nourishes and cherishes it, just as Christ does the church, because we are members of his body.

"Therefore a man shall leave his father and mother and hold fast to his wife, and the two shall become one flesh.

"This mystery is profound, and I am saying that it refers to Christ and the church. However, let each one of you love his wife as himself, and let the wife see that she respects her husband." (Ephesians 5:22–33)

The notion of wives submitting to husbands is not particularly popular in our culture, but it is instructive to genuinely study this passage.

APPLY   In what ways are Paul's instructions to husbands more challenging than those to wives?

_____

_____

_____

_____

Paul specifically calls for men to be like Jesus in their relationships with their wives. Part of that is to act as the *"head,"* or leader. Being a leader like Christ is in no way heavy-handed but involves sticking our neck out and being prepared to sacrifice anything.

The Greek language of New Testament times has several words for *love*:

- *Eros*. The idea we usually associate with love—*eros* (romantic or sexual love), from which we derive the word *erotic*—is never used in the New Testament. It is not that the Bible denigrates sexual love. In fact, an entire Old Testament book (Song of Songs) is laced with it, and it is viewed as a vital part of marriage.
- *Storge*. A second type of love, familial love—love of parents for children or children for parents—is *storge*, a word used only in a negative sense in the New Testament. In a list of sinful behaviors (Romans 1), Paul includes *astorgos*, "lacking natural affection."
- *Phileo*. A word for another type of love is *phileo*, used many times in the New Testament. This is a close love, often rendered "brotherly love." It is the type of love Jesus had (John 11:3) for Lazarus, the brother of Mary and Martha. *Phileo* is a deep, meaningful love, as demonstrated by a comment by Jesus: *"The Father himself loves* [phileo] *you, because you have loved* [phileo] *me and have believed that I came from God"* (John 16:27).
- *Agape*. The final form of love—some would say the highest form—is *agape*. It is also the most difficult for human beings to display because it is self-sacrificing and altruistic. While the expression of *phileo* or *storge* might call for giving others what they want, *agape* calls for giving what they need, implying both intimate knowledge and a sense of the larger picture of human existence.

APPLY Paul calls for husbands to *"love* [agape] *your wives just as Christ loved the church."* What does this entail?

_____

_____

_____

_____

Christ died for the church; therefore, husbands must be prepared to die for their wives.

In what ways do Prisca and Aquila display the various types of love for one another?

_____

_____

_____

_____

Their love was not selfish, however. Paul tells us that they risked their lives for him. While he does not detail the incident, it is possible this occurred in conjunction with the riot of the silversmiths in Ephesus (see Acts 19:23–41).

Word Study
HOW DO I LOVE THEE

Agape love calls for giving what others need, implying both an intimate knowledge of the other and a sense of the larger picture of human existence. *Agape* is the kind of love God displays toward people.

"For God so loved the world, that he gave his only Son, that whoever believes in him should not perish but have eternal life" (John 3:16).

"So we have come to know and to believe the love that God has for us. God is love, and whoever abides in love abides in God, and God abides in him." (1 John 4:16).

HOW COMMITTED AM I?

ecause the life of Prisca and Aquila contains so many powerful lessons, this application unit is unusually long. You may want to divide it into two days.

📖 Read the following passages about Prisca and Aquila.
Acts 18:1–3
Acts 18:18–19
Acts 18:26
Romans 16:3–5
1 Corinthians 16:19 (written from Ephesus)
2 Timothy 4:19 (written to Ephesus)

From these passages, we learn the following about Prisca and Aquila. Consider each and respond to the questions.

1. They worked together as a couple.

In what ways can married couples uniquely demonstrate their commitment to the principles of the gospel?

_____

_____

_____

_____

What happens to your service to Christ when you are in conflict with your spouse?

_____

_____

_____

2. They were willing to go anywhere to serve the gospel.

Rome to Corinth to Ephesus to Rome to Ephesus—some may be surprised by the amount of travel Aquila and Prisca experienced, supposing that such relocations would have been unusual in the ancient world. While it is true that most people were born, lived, and died within the same city, others traveled extensively. It was common, for example, for the sons of Roman citizens to be sent to tourist attractions as part of their education, and other citizens traveled to major events, such as the Poseidian Games just outside of Corinth. Sea travel was relatively safe in the first century and not particularly expensive. The Roman navy had cleaned most of the privates out of the Mediterranean a century earlier, and passage aboard cargo ships (if you were willing to endure open-air accommodations on the deck) was cheap and easy to find. If you were motivated to travel, as early Christians certainly were to spread the gospel, such travel would not be unusual.

Within the past few years, my wife and I had separate opportunities to be part of mission teams—she on a house-building trip to Honduras, me on a house-gutting Katrina relief trip to the New Orleans area. Both were profoundly impactful experiences. Not all Christians are called to missions, particularly foreign missions, and of course, one- and two-week excursions can't really compare with the kind of wholesale relocations Aquila and Prisca experienced. But getting out of your comfort zone and being willing to serve God in unfamiliar locales can produce genuine growth.

What opportunities are you aware of to serve outside of your comfort zone?

_____

_____

_____

If you haven't taken advantage of such opportunities, what prevents you?

_____

_____

_____

Of course, mission need not carry us afar. Are there close-to-home opportunities such as feeding the poor, visiting the sick, or helping victims of natural disasters in which you could participate? There are usually many in every community.

_____

_____

_____

3. They practiced extreme hospitality.

Aquila and Prisca opened their home on numerous occasions. They hosted Paul for eighteen months during his first visit to Corinth, and we can imagine (although we're not told so) that Timothy and Silas also stayed with them. While their tent-making vocation would place them in the middle class of society, their home probably was not large, so the presence of others would have impinged significantly on their privacy. In fact, like the vast majority of people, Prisca and Aquila may have lived in apartments (*insulae*). Furthermore, from Paul's letters, we know they hosted churches in their home in both Ephesus (1 Corinthians 16:19) and Rome (Romans 16:3).

We read in Acts 2:42–47 that the earliest Christians did not consider their possessions to be theirs alone. Is your home open to others? How could you improve your hospitality and provide service to others?

Is your home open to others? How could you improve your hospitality and provide service to others?

_____

_____

_____

Jesus provided a wonderful model for circles of relationships. Within His large group of followers, He had a special relationship with His twelve chosen disciples. Within the twelve, He was closest to Peter, John, and James. It is healthy for each of us to emulate such circles. Large groups are great for many things, but it is essential to have close relationships with people we trust and with whome we can share ourselves.

Do you have such relationships? If not, put together a plan to develop them:

_____

_____

_____

4. They were prepared to risk anything for the gospel.

In Romans 16:4 Paul tells us that Aquila and Prisca *"risked their necks for my life."* The literal meaning of the word translated "risk" (*hupotithemi*) is "to lay down." This is not some trivial willingness to put oneself in possible danger but a very real act of selfless protection of another. We don't know exactly what happened, but Paul's comment suggests that were it not for Prisca and Aquila, he would have died. We know that Paul faced a number of threats during his ministry, but perhaps the most dangerous was the riot of the silversmiths in Ephesus. Luke tells us that the crowd was *"enraged"* (Acts 19:28) and that the town clerk advised them they should *"do nothing rash"* (Acts 19:36). Faced with a serious loss of income because of Paul's condemnation of the idols they produced, the crowd of silversmiths, joined by others, appears to have been in the mood for a lynching. Perhaps Aquila and Prisca protected Paul at this time at their own peril.

In addition, their move from Rome to Corinth represented a considerable risk. Corinth, the center of immoral Diana worship and as carnal a city as existed in the empire, would seem a hostile environment for the moral imperatives of the gospel. If Aquila and Prisca made that decision as Christians, which I believe is likely, it is a courageous one that affirms their commitment to Christ Jesus.

American Christians sometimes like to point to some public incidents, such as the removal of the Ten Commandments from public buildings, as examples of persecution, but the fact is that we really have no understanding of *real* persecution. The fastest-growing churches are in Asia and Africa, where persecution, included imprisonment and even death, are very real.

Really think about this: what would you be unwilling to sacrifice for the gospel? Your job? Your family? Your children? Your home? Your life?

_____

_____

_____

_____

What gets in the way of your total commitment to God?

_____

_____

_____

_____

American Christians like to point to some public incidents, such as the removal of the Ten Commendments from public buildings, as examples of persecution, but the fact is that we have no understanding of real persecution.

5. They were bold in protecting sound doctrine but discrete in their correction.

When Apollos came to Ephesus, he was unfamiliar with Christian baptism, knowing *"only the baptism of John"* (Acts 18:25; a baptism of repentance but not of associating with Christ Jesus). Prisca and Aquila must have recognized Apollos's potential as an effective preacher of the gospel, so they took him aside and *"explained to him the way of God more accurately"* (v. 26). Too often today, Christians are willing to overlook inaccuracies from a powerful teacher, perhaps believing that an inaccurate message is better than no message at all. On the other hand, it is notable that Aquila and Prisca took Apollos aside to teach him. They did not challenge him in front of the non-believers he was addressing, showing that they were very sensitive to the need for Christians to remain united.

Identifying correct biblical teaching first requires a familiarity with Scripture. What is your Bible reading plan? If you don't have one, consider creating one now.

_____

_____

_____

_____

You probably can't be familiar with every word of the Bible, nor is that essential to living a full and complete Christian life, but there are certainly some essential elements of correct doctrine. What beliefs and practices would you list as essential to being a Christian?

_____

_____

_____

Have you heard Christians teach things that are contrary to these essential beliefs and practices? If so, what did you do about it?

_____

_____

_____

_____

Are there additional beliefs and practices about which you feel strongly but which may not be essential to being a Christian? What are these, and what is your attitude toward those who believe or act differently?

_____

_____

_____

6. They were reliable and trustworthy.

The term *sunergos sunergos* that serves as the basis of this Bible study implies that Paul considered Prisca and Aquila his equals in evangelizing the world and shepherding the church. He brought them to Ephesus to establish the church, he may have sent them back to Rome to help the church, and he may have even asked them to return to Ephesus to assist Timothy. Between Corinth and Ephesus, Aquila and Prisca spent at least three years working alongside Paul, and Paul's greeting suggests a distinct personal warmth. It must have been very difficult for them to remain in Ephesus when Paul sailed for Syria. It must have been even more difficult for them to return to Rome.

Think about a person in whom you have complete confidence. What are the characteristics of this person that make him or her trustworthy?

_____

_____

_____

As Christians, we are called to rely on God in all situations, but people play a vital role in God's plan. Paul writes, "Therefore, we are ambassadors for Christ, God making his appeal through us. We implore you on behalf of Christ, be reconciled to God" (2 Corinthians 5:20). Ambassadors have the duty to represent their country's administration faithfully, regardless of personal opinions.

How can you be a better ambassador for Christ?

_____

_____

_____

This truly remarkable couple was probably quite ordinary before they encountered the gospel. Through their association with other believers and their devotion to God, they accomplished extraordinary things. They were part of the earliest churches in three of the most important cities in the Roman world. Their example teaches us that God can use our ordinary lives to accomplish extraordinary things.

2

Aristarchus
Perseverance Under Fire

Aristarchus was a Macedonian from Thessalonica, one of Paul's most successful stops on his second missionary journey. His name, meaning "best ruler," suggests he came from a family of some standing in the community, although it is also possible that he was given this name when he converted to Christianity, a fairly common practice among early Christians.

During his first missionary journey, on which they would later meet Aristarchus, Paul and Barnabas ventured into the Roman provinces of Pamphylia and Galatia in what is now central Turkey, gaining many converts and facing intense opposition in Pisidian Antioch, Iconium, Lystra, and Derbe (Acts 13:13–14:24).

Put Yourself In Their Shoes
ARISTARCHUS

Aristarchus was a Greek from Thessalonica whose name means "best ruling."

Aristarchus probably met Paul in about AD 51 when Paul visited Thessalonica during his first missionary journey.

"Epaphras, my fellow prisoner in Christ Jesus, sends greetings to you, and so do Mark, Aristarchus, Demas, and Luke, my fellow workers." (Philemon 23–24)

Aristarchus

DAY ONE

ON THE ROAD WITH PAUL

I f you have not looked at Luke's account of the Asian portion of Paul's first missionary journey recently (Acts 13:13–14:26), read it now and respond to the following questions.

In Pisidian Antioch, as in other cities he visited, Paul first preached the gospel in the synagogues (13:14). Why would it be important for him to do so?

_____

_____

_____

Did You Know?
SYNAGOGUE

Archaeological and literary evidence proves that the synagogue was a well-established institution in Judea and the cities of the Diaspora (scattering of the Jews), but scholars are divided over its origins. There appear to have been two different kinds of synagogues in the first century—one a public town-assembly hall and the other a semipublic voluntary association (such as the synagogue of the Freedmen in Acts 6:9). According to Josephus and Philo (early Jewish historians), in addition to Torah reading (the primary activity), synagogues could function as council halls, archives, treasuries, hostels, and dining facilities. The common architectural element was a main hall with chairs or benches lining three or four of the walls with empty space in the center of the room, an ideal design for the typical readings, teaching, and discussion conducted at a synagogue.

Paul never forgot Jesus was the promised Messiah of the Jews. They had the necessary background teaching to understand God's plan, and Paul certainly hoped his efforts in the synagogues would provide each church a foundation of disciples.

Peter and Paul are the central figures in Luke's account of the New Testament church, and he records speeches by both.

📖 Read Acts 2:14–36; 13:16–41.

In the chart below, compare and contrast Paul's message to the one preached by Peter on the day of Pentecost.

	Peter (Acts 2:14-36)	Paul (Acts 13:16-41)
Audience and setting		
Use of Scripture		
Tone		
Testimony about Jesus		
Call to action		

In both Pisidian Antioch (Acts 13:45) and Iconium (Acts 14:2), the gospel message divided people, as it will in other places. When we read *"the Jews incited"* (13:50), it may seem that all Jews opposed Paul, but this was not the case at all. Many, if not most, of the initial believers in each city were Jews.

 Why do you think the gospel is so divisive?

_____

_____

_____

Jesus spoke of this divisiveness during His ministry as well. Take a look at the strong words of Jesus in Matthew 10:34–38. What is Jesus saying about following Him?

_____

_____

_____

_____

In modern day Christianity, it is easy for us to forget that becoming a disciple of Jesus could be very uncomfortable. In a fallen world, there are many who would rather maintain the status quo than recognize the reality of a spiritual realm. Accepting the fact of the man Jesus requires a response.

APPLY What is your understanding of the phrase *"take [up] his cross"* in verse 38?

_____

_____

_____

I have occasionally heard some refer to something relatively trivial like acne or bad hair as his or her cross to bear. We should never forget that in Jesus' time, the cross was a grotesque symbol of execution. Jesus calls us to nothing less than the readiness to suffer the kind of persecution—even death—that He and His disciples faced.

When Paul healed a crippled man in Lystra, the crowd thought he and Barnabas were gods (Acts 14:8-19). Zeus (Jupiter) was the chief god of Greek and Roman polytheistic religion, while Hermes (Mercury) was only a messenger god.

Why do you think Barnabas was hailed as Zeus and Paul only as Hermes?

_____

_____

_____

The people obviously recognized Paul as the principle spokesman for the traveling evangelists. The Lystrans had hailed Paul and Barnabas as gods, yet very soon thereafter, the people stoned them and left them for dead.

How do you account for such a radical change?

_____

_____

_____

People don't like to be fooled, particularly when the foolishness is their own. Having been excited about the prospect of a visit by Zeus and Hermes, they lashed out irrationally when their own assumptions were contradicted.

"And whoever does not take his cross and follow me is not worthy of me."

Matthew 10:38

Did You Know?
ZEUS

In Greek mythology, Zeus is the king of the gods, the ruler of Mount Olympus, and the god of the sky and thunder. A well-preserved statue, now housed in the Athens National Archaeological Museum, is believed to be Zeus, although because the weapon once in the right hand is missing, some scholars suggest it may be Poseidon instead. The people of Lystra momentarily believed Paul was Zeus come down from the heavens.

Note that Paul and Barnabas retraced their steps back from Derbe through Lystra, Iconium, and Pisidian Antioch (14:21–22). What does this demonstrate about Paul and Barnabas?

_____

_____

_____

Paul and Barnabas were not hit-and-run evangelists. They returned to cities because they knew the fledgling churches would need care and encouragement.

APPLY Acts also records that Paul and Barnabas appointed elders (presbyters) in each city (14:23). Why would this be important?

_____

_____

_____

Paul and Barnabas could not continue to nurse each young church indefinitely. Their survival depended upon full-time shepherds who knew their city and its people well.

SUPERNATURAL EXPERIENCES

After Barnabas and Paul returned to Syrian Antioch from the Jerusalem Council (Acts 15:1–29), Barnabas suggested they return to the churches they had established, but they differed sharply about bringing John Mark, who had left them in Perga (Acts 13:13). Barnabas therefore took Mark on a separate mission back to Cyprus, while Paul chose Silas to accompany him (Acts 15:36–40).

How could Paul and Barnabas, who had shared so many hardships together during their first mission, part ways over John Mark?

_____

_____

_____

Frankly, Paul's estrangement from Barnabas has always bothered me. After the incident, Barnabas, who had played such a pivotal role, virtually disappears from the biblical record. On the surface, it's easy to blame Paul's sometimes rigid standards for others and himself, but it's impossible to draw conclusions from Luke's narrative. On the other hand, this is one of those details supporting the validity of the New Testament—somewhat embarrassing stories a propagandist would certainly omit.

Paul returned through Galatia, adding young Timothy to his team in Lystra (Acts 16:1–3). Paul had just won a great victory for freedom at the Jerusalem Council when James, apparently convinced by Peter, released Gentile Christians from adherence to Jewish law and specifically from the circumcision requirements.

Why then would Paul insist that Timothy be circumcised (Acts 16:3)?

_____

_____

_____

The reason for Timothy's circumcision probably relates to his heritage. Timothy's father was Greek, but his mother (Eunice) was a Jew, making Timothy a Jew who should have been circumcised eight days after his birth. Paul remained proud of his Jewish heritage throughout his life, and he probably didn't want any controversy to arise over associating with an uncircumcised Jew.

Paul apparently planned to proceed to the province of Asia (western Turkey), but the Holy Spirit somehow forbade him, so he changed his plans and headed to Bithynia (northern Turkey, on the Black Sea). But he was again dissuaded by the Spirit, so the team proceeded to Troas on the Aegean coast (Acts 16:6–8). Apparently, in Troas Paul met Luke, the Greek physician who was to become the author of a Gospel and the book of Acts. More important to his immediate future, Paul also received a vision of a man calling him to help those in Macedonia. Paul and his team therefore found passage across the Aegean and proceeded to Philippi and then to Thessalonica.

Paul was a man of many spiritual experiences—visions, dreams, and visitations. Most obvious, of course, is his Damascus Road conversion experience (Acts 9:1–19), when he was confronted by the risen Jesus. Take a look at the partial list of Paul's spiritual encounters in the chart below and explain how each contributed to Paul's development and God's purposes.

"Now as he went on his way, he approached Damascus, and suddenly a light from heaven flashed around him."

Acts 9:3

PAUL'S SPIRITUAL ENCOUNTERS

Stephen's execution Acts 7:55-59	
Damascus Road Galatians 1:15-17; Acts 22:6-22	
Thorn in the flesh 2 Corinthians 12:7-9	
Missionary commission Acts 13:1-3	
Macedonian call Acts 16:9-10	
Corinthian vision Acts 18:9-11	
Agabus's warning Acts 21:10-11	
Going to Rome Acts 23:10-11	
Shipwreck Acts 27:21-26	

📖 Read Paul's comments about supernatural experiences in Colossians 2:18 and 1 Timothy 4:1. How do we know when such experiences are real and from God?

_____

_____

_____

Several years ago, while driving across rural Arkansas late at night en route to my daughter's college, I picked up one of the many Christian radio stations in the South and heard snippets (the reception was poor) of a sermon by Charles Stanley in which he discussed this very question. The only point I remember is Stanley's suggestion that God doesn't ask us to do things we already want to do. One virtually sure test may therefore be how welcome God's message is. We have no record of Paul's feelings about the Macedonian call, but we do know a trip across the Aegean wasn't his original intent.

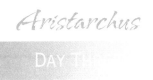

GOD FEARERS

In Thessalonica, as was his regular practice, Paul first preached in the synagogue, and Luke reports that some Jews, many devout Greeks, and _"not a few of the leading women"_ (Act 17:4) were persuaded by Paul's message and converted, stirring up jealousy among some other Jews. Even though he is not mentioned at this juncture, it seems likely that Aristarchus was among these early devout Greeks who became Christian. He was probably what is often referred to as a lover, fearer, or worshipper of God in New Testament.

📖 Read about some of these people in Acts 10 (Cornelius); 16:14 (Lydia); 18:7 (Titius Justus).

📖 Read Acts 17:1–10; then answer the following questions about the passage.

What was Paul's approach in preaching in the synagogue?

_____

_____

_____

After Paul used the Jewish Scriptures to make his case for Jesus, why were some Jews jealous?

_____

_____

_____

Nothing annoys some people as much as the success of those they oppose. How did the jealous Jews attempt to silence Paul and Silas?

_____

_____

_____

A common tactic against Paul, one we will see repeated later, was to try to convince Roman authorities that he threatened the peace of the city. Provincial governors and other officials were charged primarily with keeping order. By accusing Paul and his associates of *"acting against the decrees of Caesar"* and claiming *"there is another king,"* they hoped to capitalize on the paranoia of provincial authorities. The tactic often backfired, however, when the Romans viewed the Jewish rabble-rousers as the real source of whatever problems existed.

Aristarchus may well have been among the brothers who, along with Jason, were dragged before the city authorities and accused. Jason apparently posted bail for the group, and they immediately urged Paul and Silas to leave Thessalonica. Luke does not mention Aristarchus at this time, so he may have remained with the fledgling church in Thessalonica, although a later comment by Luke (Acts 19:29) suggests that he, along with others, may have accompanied Paul.

With Silas and Timothy, Paul went on to Berea, where Thessalonian Jews stirred up crowds against him. Berean brothers spirited him out of town again, conducting him to Athens while Silas and Timothy remained behind, later joining him in Corinth (Acts 17:10–18:5). Paul remained in Corinth about eighteen months, finally leaving with Aquila and Priscilla. After a brief stopover in Ephesus, he continued on to Caesarea and Antioch, completing his second missionary journey (Acts 18:19–22). The Antioch church sponsored Paul's missions, and he undoubtedly reported the successful introduction of the gospel in Europe before leaving on his third journey. Once again, he began by traveling through Galatia to strengthen the churches there, but his mind must have been set on his return to Ephesus, the most important city in the large Roman province of Asia (western Turkey) and a major commercial, financial, and religious center.

SEIZED BY A MOB

Aristarchus

DAY FOUR

We first encounter Aristarchus by name in Ephesus. Luke refers to him and Gaius (also a Macedonian) as *"Paul's companions in travel"* (Acts 19:29). What does this suggest to you?

_____

_____

_____

I suspect these men had been with Paul since his first visit to Thessalonica. When Paul left Antioch on his second journey, he seems to have planned to go to Ephesus from Galatia, so the Antioch church would not have known of his foray into Greece. Bringing new Christians from there to testify to his sponsors would have provided proof of his success and been a source of encouragement. Whenever Aristarchus joined Paul as a traveling companion, we know he was in Ephesus during the riot of the silversmiths.

Miniatures like this one depicting the famous Alexandria lighthouse were favored souvenirs for wealthy Romans visiting famous sites around the Roman world. Craftsmen who fashioned such gimcrack depended on sales for their living.

PAUL'S PRISON EPISTLES

Philippians, Colossians, and Ephesians, as well as 1 Timothy, 2 Timothy, and Philemon are traditionally considered to have been written during Paul's imprisonment in Rome. From internal evidence, there is no question these letters were written from prison, but some biblical scholars question the site, particularly in the case of Colossians and Philemon. Some propose Paul and other Christians were placed in some sort of protective custody after the riot of the silversmiths in Ephesus. The most compelling case for this theory is the presence of Onesimus, a runaway slave. It is unlikely, some claim, that Onesimus would have had the resources to flee to Rome. Ephesus, on the other hand, was only about a hundred-mile journey on the fine Roman roads. Tradition could be wrong, but it doesn't really matter.

📖 Read Acts 19:24–41; then answer the following questions about the passage. Why was Demetrius concerned about Paul's preaching in Ephesus?

_____

_____

_____

This was primarily an economic issue for Demetrius—Paul was apparently taking money out of his pocket. What evidence suggests Gaius and Aristarchus were in real danger?

_____

_____

_____

Mobs can be very dangerous. Social psychologists have found mob behavior tends to be more extreme than that of the mob's individual members because of the anonymity provided and the diffusion of responsibility. This kind of anonymity also contributes to road rage today. Luke reports this crowd was filled with rage and threw the city into confusion.

Why did Paul want to get involved in such a dangerous situation?

_____

_____

_____

Paul knew the crowd's anger was aimed at his activities, and he always accepted personal responsibility for his actions.

📖 Read Acts 17:5–9; 18:12–17.

How do the actions of the Ephesus town clerk (Greek *grammateus*, "scribe") compare to those of the city authorities in Thessalonica and Corinth?

_____

_____

_____

While officials in each city may have been disturbed by Paul and other Christians, their primary concern was defusing the situation to maintain public order. It is curious that a town clerk rather than a higher-ranking official addressed the crowd in Ephesus. Perhaps the governor was out of town or didn't have the nerve to face the mob. After two hours, someone had to step up, and this unnamed scribe may have drawn the short straw among the city's lower functionaries.

In Colossians 4:10 Paul refers to Aristarchus as his *"fellow prisoner,"* and in 2 Corinthians 11:23 Paul reports he has suffered *"far more imprisonments"* (than other apostles). Since he wrote 2 Corinthians before his only recorded incarcerations in Caesarea and Rome, some scholars suggest he and Aristarchus were placed under protective custody in Ephesus following the riot.

📖 Read Acts 20:1.

Why do you think Paul decided to leave Ephesus at this time?

_____

_____

_____

Paul may have simply decided he'd spent enough time in the city. After all, it was his longest stay in one place since he had first been commissioned by the Antioch church. I suspect, however, he left to further the teaching of the gospel in Ephesus.

How might Paul's departure have improved the opportunities for the Ephesian Christians to teach people about Jesus?

_____

_____

_____

Everything Paul did was related to spreading the gospel. Because the complaints of Demetrius and the other craftsmen were centered on Paul, his departure would have defused the tension in the city and improved the environment for evangelism.

Aristarchus was one of a large group of companions who accompanied Paul to Greece, where he remained for three months. Deciding to visit the Macedonian churches, Paul sent most of his contingent, including Aristarchus, to Troas to wait for him (Acts 20:1–6). In Troas, Aristarchus was probably a witness to Paul's healing of Eutychus, the young man who fell asleep during a lengthy sermon by Paul and fell from a third-story window (Acts 20:7–12).

Aristarchus must have continued to travel with Paul on his journey to deliver the collection gathered by the Macedonian churches to the Jerusalem church, which was suffering a major famine. In Jerusalem Paul again faced grave danger, and Aristarchus was there.

📖 Read Acts 21:27–22:23.

In Ephesus, Paul had aroused the ire of secular craftsmen, but their goal was probably to have him banished from the city. What incensed some Jews in Jerusalem so much they wanted to kill him?

_____

_____

To the Jews of Jerusalem, Paul was the ultimate traitor—a Jew preaching a blasphemous doctrine to Gentiles! To first-century Jews, Gentiles were often viewed as the scum of the earth—people with whom God's chosen people were not even allowed to associate, although this was certainly a perversion of God's mission for his people. Now here was Paul claiming their God had personally sent him to the Gentiles. Only Paul's Roman citizenship saved him from a band of conspirators plotting his death (Acts 23:12–13).

"I have become all things to all people, that by all means I might save some."

I Corinthians 9:22

DID PAUL BREAK THE LAW?

The immediate source of the anger directed toward Paul in Jerusalem involved a point of Jewish law. Some charged him with bringing Trophimus, an Ephesian Gentile, into the temple and by doing so *"[defiling] this holy place"* (Acts 21:28). Gentiles were not altogether prohibited from visiting Herod's temple in Jerusalem, but they could not go past the outer court. According to Josephus, signs at the gates into the inner courts—written in Hebrew, Greek, and Latin—warned any Gentile or unclean person from proceeding on the threat of death.

The charge was clearly a fabrication, because Paul knew the law well, having been a student of Gamaliel, the most respected Jewish teacher of his time (Acts 22:3), and he maintained his respect for his Jewish roots throughout his life. Furthermore, Paul had just completed a seven-day period of ritual purification. What could he possibly have gained from violating the law?

Aristarchus

DAY FIVE

For the next two years, Paul remained in custody under two Roman governors. Held in Caesarea Maritima, the great port city built by the Romans, he was at least initially permitted visitors by Governor Felix (Acts 24:23). When Portius Festus succeeded Felix, he must have been perplexed by Paul's incarceration, because he sought to resolve the case. After investigation, he seemed to have been prepared to release Paul, but Paul insisted on making a defense before the emperor in Rome.

Luke reports Aristarchus was with them when Paul departed Caesarea aboard an Adramyttium ship bound first for Lycia. Consequently, Aristarchus almost certainly experienced the shipwreck at Malta, witnessed Paul's survival of a venomous snake bite, and proceeded to Italy with Paul and Luke aboard a second Alexandrian ship (Acts 27:2–28:14).

AM I PERSEVERING?

The Bible contains just five brief allusions to Aristarchus (Acts 19:29; 20:4; 27:2; Colossians 4:10; Philemon 24), and his name is unknown to most Christians, yet even the scant information we have testifies to an incredible life of service and loyalty. He traveled with Paul for at least seven years and perhaps as many as thirteen. He was jailed for his faith and earned Paul's highest acclaim as *sunergos sunergos* ("fellow worker"). Along with Paul, he visited dozens of early churches and undoubtedly contributed to the spread of the gospel and the encouragement of the earliest Christians.

Consider the following events in Aristarchus's life:

AD 51	Probably converted at Thessalonica during Paul's second missionary journey. Possibly among the Christians seized by a mob almost immediately thereafter (Acts 17:4–6).
AD 54	In Ephesus taken by another angry mob and dragged into the theater, where the mob chanted to their pagan god for two hours.
AD 56	In Jerusalem, where yet another mob set on Paul and a group of conspirators sought to assassinate the apostle.
AD 57-59	Probably remained in Caesarea throughout Paul's incarceration, perhaps ministering to his needs.
AD 59-60	With Paul under Roman guard, experiencing the harrowing voyage to Rome, including the shipwreck on Malta.
AD 60	Arrived in Rome, where Paul remained in custody pending a trial before the emperor.

After each of these events, Aristarchus had an opportunity to abandon Paul, who clearly attracted a lot of trouble. He could have remained in his home in Thessalonica. After the riot of the silversmiths in Ephesus, a relatively short trip across the Aegean would have taken Aristarchus back to

Thessalonica. When Paul left Ephesus, he probably passed through Thessalonica twice, and Aristarchus could have dropped out then. After Paul was seized in Jerusalem, Aristarchus could have found his way home. When the ship left Caesarea, it first docked in Lycia, and Aristarchus could have headed home from there.

At each of these crossroads, Aristarchus could have concluded he'd done enough, and he may have thought about a prudent separation from Paul. Returning to his home in Thessalonica, he could have lived quietly, serving the church there in a variety of ways.

APPLY Have you ever faced challenges during your Christian life when you had to decide between a difficult course and an easier one? Which did you choose and why?

_____

_____

_____

_____

We have no record of any specific activity by Aristarchus during his many years with Paul—no speeches, baptisms, miracles. What do you think his role was?

_____

_____

_____

Whatever he did during his travels with Paul, there is one word that certainly describes Aristarchus—*persevering*. He remained loyal to Christ Jesus and Paul through a series of extraordinarily challenging events. He got his co-worker label the hard way—he *earned* it!

Perseverance (or endurance) is a key concept in the Christian life. The Greek terms are *hupomonē* (perseverance) and *hupomenō* (persevering), which appear at least thirty-eight times in the New Testament. Jesus used it in his discussion of the parable of the sower.

📖 Read Luke 8:4–15.

Jesus concludes his explanation of the parable by saying, *"As for that in the good soil, they are those who, hearing the word, hold it fast in an honest and good heart, and bear fruit with patience* [hupomonē]" (v. 15).

APPLY What does this saying tell you about being a Christian?

_____

_____

_____

Being a Christian isn't supposed to be easy or comfortable. Bearing fruit (developing the characteristics of Jesus in ourselves and making new disciples) requires the full meaning of *hupomonē*—patient endurance. In this sense, endurance is not putting up with something, it is cheerful waiting with hope and confidence.

APPLY Why would cheerfulness and patience be important in perseverance?

_____
_____
_____
_____

Every attitude we hold and every action we take is a potential witness to those who do not yet know Christ Jesus. Most people endure unpleasant circumstances with something less than cheerfulness and patience, but by exhibiting these qualities while we wait, we invite others to ask us important questions.

📖 Read Luke 21:16–19.

What role does Jesus say *hupomonē* (patience, endurance; v. 19) plays?

_____
_____
_____

According to Jesus, bricks of *hupomonē* pave the road to salvation, but patient endurance (steadfastness) is not a natural characteristic in most people, particularly in America. Our fast-paced consumer society constantly tells us we can have what we want and we can have it now. Furthermore, it is comfortable to be a cultural Christian in America, robbing us of the kind of dramatic opportunities to develop the perseverance Aristarchus and other early Christians faced. James wrote,

> *"Count it all joy, my brothers, when you meet trials of various kinds, for you know that the testing of your faith produces steadfastness [hupomonē]. And let steadfastness have its full effect, that you may be perfect and complete, lacking in nothing."* (1:2–4)

In some parts of the world, our brothers and sisters face persecution similar to that endured in the early church, even to the point of death, but our challenges are more subtle—the person who cuts us off in traffic, the political commentator mocking Christians, the rough language in the workplace, the pervasive tolerance of sin in our society, the perverse images in our media.

APPLY What opportunities do you see around you to develop *hupomonē*?

_____
_____
_____
_____
_____

Maturing as a Christian requires effort.

📖 Read 2 Peter 1:5–10. If we fail to develop *hupomonē* (steadfastness, endurance, perseverance), what do we risk?

_____

_____

_____

_____

_____

Paul tells us we are saved by grace through faith (Ephesians 2:8), but Peter contends faith alone cannot produce the growth that makes us complete and effective. He calls us to *"make every effort"* to go beyond faith to virtue, knowledge, self-control, steadfastness (*hupomonē*), godliness, brotherly affection, and love.

A week or two spent in a detailed study of *hupomonē* in the New Testament would be beneficial for all of us. If you want to do that, here's a list of some *hupomonē / hupomenō* passages:

Matthew 10:22	2 Corinthians 12:12	James 1:3
Matthew 24:13	Colossians 1:11	James 1:12
Mark 13:13	1 Thessalonians 1:3	James 5:11
Luke 8:15	2 Thessalonians 1:4	1 Peter 2:20
Luke 21:19	1 Timothy 6:11	2 Peter 1:6
Romans 2:7	2 Timothy 2:10–12	Revelation 1:9
Romans 5:3–4	2 Timothy 3:10	Revelation 2:2–3
Romans 8:25	Titus 2:2	Revelation 2:19
Romans 12:12	Hebrews 10:32	Revelation 3:10
Romans 15:4–5	Hebrews 10:36	Revelation 13:10
1 Corinthians 13:7	Hebrews 12:1	Revelation 14:12
2 Corinthians 1:6	Hebrews 12:2–3	
2 Corinthians 6:4	Hebrews 12:7	

As we look to Scripture for examples of faith, commitment, loyalty, and courage, we need look no further than Aristarchus. By most accounts, he would be considered a minor character, but his life was one of major discipleship and perseverance. In his last letter to Timothy, Paul writes, *"I have fought the good fight, I have finished the race, I have kept the faith"* (2 Timothy 4:7). Aristarchus could say the same thing.

Postscript on Aristarchus
Because Luke ends his narrative of the early church with Paul's house arrest in Rome, awaiting an audience with Emperor Nero, we have no authoritative account of Paul's fate, nor of Aristarchus's. Roman Catholic tradition holds that Aristarchus was the first bishop (overseer) of Thessalonica, but if he was Paul's constant companion from the apostle's first visit to Thessalonica (about AD 51) until his arrival in Rome (about AD 60), this seems unlikely since Aristarchus would have spent very little time in his home city. Furthermore, in his *Ecclesiastical History* (about AD 320), Eusebius Pamphilius fails to cite Aristarchus as a bishop of Thessalonica even though Eusebius carefully chronicles the bishops of every major city from apostolic to his time.

A second Roman Catholic tradition suggests that Aristarchus was executed along with Paul in Rome. Many biblical scholars believe that Paul was released from his Roman imprisonment around AD 62 and preceded on an unrecorded missionary journey to Spain. That Paul targeted Spain for a mission is documented by his own comments in Romans 15:24, 28. This account of Paul's later life suggests that after the Spanish mission, he proceeded on a farewell tour of churches in Greece and Asia before returning to Rome, where he was again imprisoned (the occasion of his second letter to Timothy) and subsequently executed as a scapegoat for the Great Fire of Rome in AD 64. If this chronology is accurate, Artistarchus's proven loyalty suggests he would have continued with the apostle, and as a close associate, his execution would be likely. But when Paul writes what was likely his last letter while he sat in a Roman prison, he tells us that *"Luke alone is with me"* (2 Timothy 4:11). We have no clue of Aristarchus's fate.

3

Euodia and Syntyche
Working Out Differences

To the casual Bible reader, the most surprising inclusion on the list of Paul's co-workers must surely be Euodia and Syntyche, who go down in Christian history as women who couldn't get along. Their conflict threatened the unity of the church in Philippi, and we never learn if they worked things out, but it is important to understand what Paul said about them and what is implied by the lengths he went to encourage them to put aside whatever difference they had. Typically, commentaries suggest Paul wanted them to agree, but his comments may suggest something slightly different.

Philippi was a major Roman colony in the province of Macedonia (northern Greece). Paul first visited there on his second missionary journey after his Macedonian vision (read Acts 15:40–16:12 for background). The first convert to Christianity in Europe was an Asian fabric dealer named Lydia, with whom Paul and his party stayed for a time. Typical of Paul, he soon ran afoul of some local residents, got beaten, and ended up in jail. Freed after an earthquake (and the conversion of his jailer, Acts 16:13–40), Paul soon headed south out of Philippi, but the church there was probably never far from his mind. He appreciated the Philippian believers for a number of reasons, one of which is that they alone took it upon themselves to provide support for him. During his third missionary journey, after a lengthy stay in Ephesus, Paul returned to Macedonia before sailing to Judea (Acts 20:1–6).

Put Yourself In Their Shoes
EUODIA AND SYNTYCHE

Euodia (*yoo-od-EE-ah*) "fine traveling" or "fragrant"

Syntyche (*soon-TOO-khay*)—"an accident" or "fortunate"

Both were Christian women from Philippi. They met Paul during one of his visits to the city during his second or third missionary journeys. Perhaps one or both were among the women at the riverside (Acts 16:13).

"I entreat Euodia and I entreat Syntyche to agree in the Lord. Yes, I ask you also, true companion, help these women, who have labored side by side with me in the gospel together with Clement and the rest of my fellow workers, whose names are in the book of life." (Philippians 4:2–3)

During Paul's first imprisonment in Rome (about AD 61–63), the Philippian church apparently heard of his plight, gathered up some gifts for him, and dispatched Epaphroditus. Some commentators have speculated that this may have occurred during an imprisonment in Ephesus or Caesarea, but Rome appears more likely. If Paul was imprisoned in Ephesus, it was probably not long enough for the events related in his letter to the Philippian church. While we know Paul's imprisonment under Felix and Festus in Caesarea extended for a couple of years (Acts 23:23–27:1), Paul doesn't seem to have been given the same opportunity there for visitors or letter writing as he was in Rome.

Euodia and Syntyche

DAY ONE

Did You Know?

PAUL'S VISITS TO PHILIPPI

Paul visited Philippi on at least three occasions. The first came in AD 51, during his second missionary journey, when it was his first major stop in Europe and Lydia became the first European convert. The other two visits were during the third missionary journey, probably in AD 56. He traveled up and down Macedonia and Achaia after leaving Ephesus and before proceeding to Jerusalem. By Luke's accounts, none of these visits lasted more than a week or two, but Paul had a profound effect on the people of Philippi and they on him.

CONFLICT IN THE CHURCH

The impetus for Paul's letter to the church in Philippi seems to have been twofold: his gratitude to them for sending Epaphroditus with gifts (Philippians 4:18) and the news Epaphroditus must have conveyed about a conflict between Euodia and Syntyche. In fact, the bulk of the letter may be targeted at their disagreement.

What was the conflict about? Paul gives us no information about the problem Euodia and Syntyche were having, but perhaps we can draw some conclusions regarding what it was **not** about.

APPLY Do you think the issue was relatively **trivial**, like some petty argument over recipes or household chores? Why or why not? Consider what kinds of issues Paul addressed in other letters.

_____

_____

_____

_____

The issue was certainly not trivial. Paul would not have taken the time he did if it were. Furthermore, if the matter were trivial, it would never have been communicated to Paul in the first place. This was an issue that threatened the unity of the entire Philippian congregation.

APPLY Do you think the issue involved something **personal**, like some perceived insult either Euodia or Syntyche said about the other? Why or why not? Consider how Paul dealt with the issue of Philemon's escaped slave (see Philemon).

_____

_____

_____

_____

The issue was probably not personal. The letter is addressed, *"To all the saints in Christ Jesus who are at Philippi"* (1:1). As an *encyclical* letter, it would have been read publicly to the entire church. If the matter were strictly personal, it is unlikely Paul would have risked embarrassing the women before the congregation. Furthermore, that he does not delineate the subject of the conflict suggests that everyone in Philippi knew what it was. When Paul wrote to Philemon, encouraging him to accept his escaped slave Onesimus as a brother, he did so privately. He did not mention the subject in the general letter to the church in Colossae, where Philemon lived, even though the letters were written and delivered at the same time.

 Do you think the issue involved some core doctrine of Christianity? Why or why not? Consider Paul's remarks in Romans 14.

_____

_____

_____

The issue was probably not doctrinal. If the conflict between Euodia and Syntyche involved a core principle of Christianity, such as the Judaizing that dogged Paul throughout most of his Christian life, Paul surely would offered his opinion.

📖 Read Philippians 4:2. Note how Paul entreats (or depending on your translation, perhaps beseeches or exhorts) each woman individually. To make his point, Paul repeats the plea (Greek *parakaleo*, which literally means "to call to one's side") to each: *"I entreat Euodia and I entreat Syntyche."* He expects each of them to make an effort.

📖 Read Philippians 4:3.

What does Paul say that demonstrates this conflict does not directly threaten Euodia or Syntyche's salvation?

_____

_____

_____

Because Paul wrote, *"These women . . . whose names are in the book of life,"* we know he did not consider their salvation at risk. He never warned them that God was standing back with a divine eraser preparing to obliterate their names. To a degree, perhaps his apparent confidence about their salvation was because of their past service, when they *"labored side by side"* (Greek *sunathleō*, literally "wrestle in company") with him.

WOMEN AS CHURCH LEADERS

Because Paul took the time in his letter to the church in Philippi to address the conflict between Euodia and Syntyche, some commentators suggest the women were rival leaders within the church and their situation threatened the unity of the Christian community in the city.

The question of women's roles in the church is controversial in some Christian circles, and there are a number of books available on the subject.

"Therefore let us not pass judgment on one another any longer, but rather decide never to put a stumbling block or hindrance in the way of a brother."

Romans 14:13

📖 Doctrine
BOOK OF LIFE

The Book of Life contains the names of those who will enter into eternal life with God. It is not a physical book, of course, since God is not a physical being. God speaks to humans and shows us images (such as John's Revelation) in terms we can understand. There are debates about the relationship between the Book of Life described in the Old Testament and the Lamb's Book of Life in the New. These differences are not really important if we have committed to Jesus. What's important is whether we're there or not.

Euodia and Syntyche

DAY TWO

"And [Elizabeth]
exclaimed with a
loud cry, 'Blessed
are you among
women, and blessed
is the fruit of your
womb!'"

Luke 1:42

The purpose of today's lesson is not to resolve that issue but rather simply to look at the roles women played in Jesus' ministry. This will help us put some perspective on Euodia and Syntyche.

📖 Read Luke 1:39–45.

What role did Elizabeth play?

_____

_____

Elizabeth was the first person to acknowledge Jesus and all that He is and will be.

📖 Read Luke 2:36–38.

What role did Anna play?

_____

_____

In a sense, Anna could be considered the first evangelist (one who speaks about the gospel).

📖 Read Luke 10:38–42; John 11.

What do you note about Mary and Martha?

_____

_____

_____

Even Roman girls received only a rudimentary, mostly domestic education, and Jewish girls were not afforded the same opportunities to learn the Torah as boys were. Jesus, a rabbi, teaching a woman was a remarkable event. Jesus had several interactions with Mary and Martha, and their home was a frequent retreat for Him. Jesus went there for peace, comfort, and companionship.

📖 Read Matthew 15:21–28.

Why is significant about this unnamed woman?

_____

_____

"Then Jesus
answered her, 'O
woman, great is
your faith! Be it
done for you as you
desire.' And her
daughter was
healed instantly."

Matthew 15:28

The Syrophoenician (Canaanite) woman is perhaps the first Gentile to acknowledge Jesus' lordship.

📖 Read Luke 8:1–3.

What role did Joanna and Susanna play?

_____

_____

As an itinerant preacher, Jesus had no routine source of income. Rabbis frequently relied on contributions from students and benefactors, but it was highly unusual for one to be supported by women.

📖 Read the following passages about Mary Magdalene.

"There were also women looking on from a distance [at Jesus' crucifixion], among whom were Mary Magdalene, and Mary the mother of James the younger and of Joses, and Salome." (Mark 15:40)

"And Joseph bought a linen shroud, and taking him down, wrapped him in the linen shroud and laid him in a tomb that had been cut out of the rock. And he rolled a stone against the entrance of the tomb. Mary Magdalene and Mary the mother of Joses saw where he was laid." (Mark 15:46–47)

"Now on the first day of the week Mary Magdalene came to the tomb early, while it was still dark, and saw that the stone had been taken away from the tomb. So she ran and went to Simon Peter and the other disciple, the one whom Jesus loved, and said to them, 'They have taken the Lord out of the tomb, and we do not know where they have laid him.' So Peter went out with the other disciple, and they were going toward the tomb" (John 20:1–3).

"'But go, tell his disciples and Peter that he is going before you to Galilee. There you will see him, just as he told you.' And they went out and fled from the tomb, for trembling and astonishment had seized them, and they said nothing to anyone, for they were afraid" (Mark 16:7–8, a "young man" [v. 5], presumably an angel, speaking to Mary Magdalene and Mary, the mother of James and Salome [v. 1].)

"Now when [Jesus] rose early on the first day of the week, he appeared first to Mary Magdalene, from whom he had cast out seven demons" (Mark 16:9).

"Having said this, she turned around and saw Jesus standing, but she did not know that it was Jesus. Jesus said to her, 'Woman, why are you weeping? Whom are you seeking?' Supposing him to be the gardener, she said to him, 'Sir, if you have carried him away, tell me where you have laid him, and I will take him away.' Jesus said to her, 'Mary.' She turned and said to him in Aramaic, 'Rabboni!' (which means Teacher). Jesus said to her, 'Do not cling to me, for I have not yet ascended to the Father; but go to my brothers and say to them, "I am ascending to my Father and your Father, to my God and your God"'" (John 20:14–17).

"She went and told those who had been with him, as they mourned and wept. But when they heard that he was alive and had been seen by her, they would not believe it" (Mark 16:10–11).

Summarize these notable events in the life of Mary Magdalene.

_____

_____

_____

_____

_____

_____

_____

_____

> **"But go, tell his disciples and Peter that he is going before you to Galilee. There you will see him, just as he told you."**
>
> **Mark 16:7**

There is a lot of speculation about Mary Magdalene today and her relationship with Jesus, but the theories that she was His lover or wife have absolutely no basis in historical fact. The biblical record, however, reveals a startling series of special roles for her: she was present at the burial of Jesus, she discovered the empty tomb, she was directed to carry the news to the disciples, she was the first to see Jesus after his resurrection, and she delivered the good news to the disciples.

This lesson could continue to study some of the notable women mentioned in the New Testament after the Gospels. It is easy to view the New Testament as a male-dominated story, but the truth is that women are equally prominent in terms of variety if not word count. Scripture reveals them confessing, evangelizing, praying, prophesying, giving, serving, supporting, receiving forgiveness, anointing, and even announcing the resurrection. Short of specifically-designated Apostleship, there seems to be no role from which women were excluded. Considering the literal meaning of apostle as a "messenger," there were certainly women apostles in the early church.

Jesus dedicated much of his ministry to elevating the status of every oppressed and undervalued person, including women in general.

Paul was equally complimentary of the women in his ministry.

📖 Read Romans 16:1–16.

Beside Priscilla, what women does Paul cite and what does he say about them?

_____

_____

_____

Did You Know?

WOMEN IN THE EARLY CHURCH

While more men are mentioned in the New Testament than women, the number of women that are mentioned is remarkable for the times. In most parts of the Roman world, women were blocked from formal education and property ownership. Other than those listed in Romans 16, some of the notable women in the early church include Tabitha (Dorcas), in Acts 9:36–42; Lydia, in Acts 16:14–15; and Damaris, Acts 17:33–34.

Euodia and Syntyche

DAY THREE

DO I NEED TO READ GREEK TO UNDERSTAND THE NEW TESTAMENT?

The answer is an unqualified no! Nearly every translation of the Bible is a reliable rendering of the New Testament, even though there are some minor differences, none of which affect important Christian doctrines. On the other hand, to get the full flavor of the New Testament, there are many helps available, the most important of which is Strong's concordance. I don't read *koine* Greek (the language of the New Testament), but I routinely reference Strong's work and other language references.

BEING OF THE SAME MIND

📖 Read Philippians 4:2–3.

What did Paul ask of Euodia and Syntyche? What does that mean?

_____

_____

_____

Depending on your Bible version, you may read Paul entreating them to *"agree"* (ESV), *"live in harmony"* (NASB), *"be of the same mind"* (KJV), or *"stop arguing"* (CEV). There are a few places in the New Testament text where the translation from Greek to English is ambiguous (although none of those involve matters of core Christian doctrine), and this is one of those. There is a major difference between agreeing and living in harmony—people can and do live in harmony with agreeing about everything!

So what did Paul mean? He certainly knew, and so too did his hearers, if only because Epaphroditus delivered the letter after spending time with Paul. They must have thoroughly discussed the problem.

The Greek phrase is *autos* (same) *phroneo* (which, according to Strong's concordance literally means "to exercise the mind, that is, entertain or have a sentiment or opinion." Paul adds *"in the Lord"* to the phrase, inviting the women (and the rest of the congregation) to consider what is truly important. In context, Paul's admonition seems to be, "Put aside your differing opinions and focus on the Lord."

While these two verses (Philippians 4:2–3) are sometimes viewed as almost parenthetical, following Paul's great Christological statements earlier in the letter, there is considerable internal evidence that they were in fact his central purpose. Everything prior to these two verses set up Paul's plea, and the five that follow summarize.

In the first twenty-six verses of the letter, Paul wrote about his experiences and his love for the Philippian church. Writing from custody in Rome, Paul was conflicted between the prospect of death bringing him to Christ Jesus and a continued life of service.

Read Philippians 1:23–26.

Which did Paul choose and why?

_____

_____

_____

Word Study
STANDING FIRM

Another Greek word Paul uses in Philippians 1:27 is *stēcō*, which literally means "to be stationary." Paul uses *stēcō* several times (1 Corinthians 16:13; Galatians 5:1; Philippians 4:1; 1 Thessalonians 3:8; 2 Thessalonians 2:15) to encourage Christian brothers to stand firm in the Lord or in faith rather than wavering as some did then and still do today.

Apparently because of needs in Philippi, Paul wanted to continue on. What was drawing him back to Philippi? The evidence suggests it was Euodia and Syntyche.

Read Philippians 1:27.

What is the relationship between this verse and Paul's plea to Euodia and Syntyche?

_____

_____

_____

Verse 27 seems to mark the beginning of his discussion of the problem between the women. Paul used an identical word and a similar phrase in 1:27 and 4:2–3. In both, he writes about wrestling or struggling together (*sunathleō*) and practicing a sameness (*autos*) together. There is no implication that the sameness Paul calls for is complete conformity. He put this notion away definitively in Romans 14. If you think Paul is calling for conformity here, you may want to review that section of Scripture.

Read Philippians 2:1–2.

Does verse 2 help explain precisely what Paul meant when he asked Euodia and Syntyche to agree, to be of the same mind, and to live in harmony?

_____

_____

_____

Once again, Paul used the phrase *auto phroneō*, and the meaning becomes clear here by his additional comments expressed best, I believe, by the NASB:

"Being of the same mind, maintaining the same love, united in spirit, intent on one purpose." Being of the same mind does not require conformity but rather love for one another, commitment to unity, and focus on purpose. With love, unity, and purpose in place, people concentrate on the things that bind them rather than the differences. The letter continues:

> *"Do nothing from rivalry or conceit, but in humility count others more significant than yourselves. Let each of you look not only to his own interests, but also to the interests of others. Have this mind among yourselves, which is yours in Christ Jesus."* (Philippians 2:3–5)

 Do you think this is a general admonition, or does Paul have something more specific in mind?

_____

_____

_____

Doctrine
PHILIPPIANS 2:6–11

The hymn in Philippians 2:6–11 (so identified because of its poetic elements in the original Greek) has been the subject of considerable debate as to its origins and background. Some claim Old Testament foundations from Isaiah (the suffering servant), while others see Gnostic elements.

Gnosticism (from the Greek word for "knowledge") came in many flavors in pagan, Jewish, and Christian circles, but there were at least two common elements: (1) the belief that salvation came through (secret) knowledge and (2) that existence comprised of two elements—spirit (good) and matter (bad). Gnosticism became a prevalent source of Christian heresies in the second and third centuries and is making a bit of a comeback today.

It's not surprising the hymn apparently appealed to Paul because it focuses on Jesus' sacrifice, which was Paul's primary message. On the surface, the hymn is quite simple: Jesus has always existed, He is equal to God, He humbled himself and lived as a human being, God raised Him to the highest place, and He will be acknowledged by all at the end times. Every element of the hymn is reinforced elsewhere in the New Testament.

There are a number of issues Paul cites in the letter, but I suspect this one relates directly to Euodia and Syntyche because it immediately follows his first call to live in harmony. I get a distinct visual image of these two women beginning to squirm in their seats when this section was read. Some heads may even have turned furtively in their direction.

To hammer the point home, it seems, Paul calls upon the example of Christ himself using, according to many biblical scholars, an early hymn.

Read Philippians 2:6–11.

Why might Paul quote a hymn to the Philippians at this point in his letter?

_____

_____

_____

There are at least two possible reasons for the hymn. First, the Philippians were probably familiar with it—perhaps it even originated there. Second, Paul is making the point that if Jesus himself, the Son of God, could *"[make] himself nothing,"* then surely so could they (the congregation in general, and Euodia and Syntyche in particular).

Read Philippians 2:14.

With what you've read, how would you describe the problem between Euodia and Syntyche?

_____

_____

_____

We can't be sure, but I don't think the actual disagreement mattered to Paul at all. What concerned him was the attitude and resultant behavior of two influential women. Instead of displaying love, unity, and purpose, the women (and probably a significant portion of the congregation, having taken sides) were each insisting on having her own way, grumbling and complaining about the other. There may have been serious trouble in Philippi.

RECONCILIATION

Philippians is an **encyclical** letter, one intended for an entire church, and Paul deliberately addressed Euodia and Syntyche in this public way because he was calling for the entire congregation to participate in the process of reconciliation. This is undoubtedly because, while the dispute originated with the two women, the congregation was beginning to fragment into supporting factions. Having dealt with divisions in the past, Paul didn't want arguably his most beloved church to fall into the same morass.

📖 Read Philippians 2:14–15.

What is Paul's biggest concern about the dispute?

_____

_____

As I've suggested elsewhere in this study, Paul was all about spreading the gospel so as many as possible might be saved. While preaching and teaching are important evangelistic tools, Paul seems to think the most important one is the difference Christ Jesus makes in individuals. Were Euodia and Syntyche shining *"as lights in the world,"* or were they virtually indistinguishable from the pagans around them? I think the answer is apparent. Paul identified the problem and its impact. Now what about the solution?

First, as we've seen, he entreated each woman to live in harmony with the other. Second, he involved others in the process.

📖 Read Philippians 4:2–3 again.

Who does Paul ask to help Euodia and Syntyche work out their problem?

_____

_____

_____

Paul first addresses a *suzugos,* which is variously translated as *"true companion"* (ESV, NASB), *"true yokefellow"* (KJV), *"true partner"* (CEV), or *"loyal yokefellow"* (NIV). Commentators have attempted to puzzle out who this *suzugos* is, with suggestions including Silas, Lydia, Epaphroditus, Timothy, a church bishop, Paul's wife, the husband of one of the women, and a man named Sygygus (the transliteration of *suzugos*). Literally, the word *suzugos* means "co-yoked" and is used only here in the New Testament. Its root, *suzeugnumi,* is used by Jesus to refer to God's joining together of man and woman in marriage (Matthew 19:6; Mark 10:9). When Paul warned about being bound together (or yoked unequally) with unbelievers (2 Corinthians 6:14), he used an entirely different word.

Personally, I don't think Paul was referring to an individual. I think he was addressing the church in Philippi as a whole, although he gives particular responsibility to Clement. Having addressed the problem in a church letter and implying the problem goes beyond the two women, it would be natural for Paul to challenge the entire group.

If Paul considered his generation crooked and twisted, what would he think today?

Doctrine
UNEQUALLY YOKED

There are a few Bible verses that often get misquoted or misused. One example is, "Money is the root of all evil," a commonly heard saying. But the actual passage (1 Timothy 6:10) says, "The love of money is a root of all kinds of evils."

Another example is, "Do not be yoked together with unbelievers," which is used to suggest Christians should not associate with non-Christians. But the actual passage (2 Corinthians 6:14) is, "Do not be unequally yoked with unbelievers." It's not only OK to associate with non-Christians; it's what we're called to do! Paul is only advising Christians not to put themselves in a position where they are subservient to a non-Christian and might have to compromise their faith as a result.

In what sense could the church be called Paul's *"true yokefellow"*?

_____

_____

_____

Paul considers himself bound to all Christians by their common faith and purpose. Referring to them as yokefellows follows the sense of his earlier references to the church in Philippi.

Once again, the Greek term *sullambanō* implies more than simple helping. *Sullambanō* is a strong action, literally meaning "to take capture" or "to take hold together with one." Paul wants the Philippi *ekklesia* (the called-out people) to take hold together with Euodia and Syntyche. None of them can correct this problem alone—only by carrying it to Christ, with his example of humility and sacrifice, is there real hope.

Paul calls first for the women to take responsibility and correct their own attitudes. He then asks the church as a whole to carry them along to reconciliation. Finally, he asks his co-workers (probably nonresidents of Philippi) to be part of the process.

📖 Read Philippians 4:4–13.

What is Paul's prescription for addressing the problem?

_____

_____

_____

_____

In some combination, the actions of Euodia and Syntyche were not true, honorable, just, pure, loving, commendable, excellent, or (certainly) worthy of praise. By rejoicing in the Lord (v. 4) and taking everything to Him in prayer (v. 6), the anxiety (v. 6) created by the conflict will be extinguished, the church will find peace (v. 7) and the people around them will see the difference (v. 5). This is the *"secret"* Paul discovered (v. 12), and through it he learned *"I can do all things through him who strengthens me"* (v. 13). Through that understanding, the things that happened to him *"really served to advance the gospel"* (1:12). This is the lesson Paul wanted not only Euodia and Syntyche but the entire Philippian *ekklesia* to know.

> *"Finally, brothers, whatever is true, whatever is honorable, whatever is just, whatever is pure, whatever is lovely, whatever is commendable, if there is any excellence, if there is anything worthy of praise, think about these things."*
>
> **Philippians 4:8**

Euodia and Syntyche

DAY FIVE

Am I a Light in the World?

As we saw in studying Philippians this week, Paul took a proactive role in challenging the Philippian church to address and solve the problems created by the conflict between Euodia and Syntyche. He was certainly concerned about the maturation of the Christians there, but his primary desire seems to have been that they restore their unity so they could resume being a light in the city.

📖 Read Matthew 5:13–16.

What does it mean to *"let your light shine,"* and why is that important?

_____

_____

_____

Most people are not attracted to Christ Jesus by sermons or dynamic assemblies; or if they are, they're probably associating with Christianity for the wrong reasons. People are attracted to Christ Jesus by the difference they see He makes in others' lives. Conversely, people are repelled by Christians whose behavior they view as hypocritical. Part of the problem is that the church too often lays complex doctrinal formulations and quasi laws on people, things that have little to do with Christ Jesus. When church members act in contradiction to these laws or doctrines, they are viewed as hypocrites.

Because the church is populated by human beings, there will always be conflicts. The health of a church depends on how we deal with them.

What are the consequences of ignoring conflicts between church members?

_____

_____

_____

Some situations will just go away as a function of time, but most problems will fester, growing deeper and more intractable. If a conflict is sufficiently serious to require intervention, who has responsibility?

_____

_____

Everything in the church is, in one way or another, everyone's responsibility. The Christian world has seen all too often the results of autocratic church leadership. Of course, there are certainly times when leadership action is required, but more often a conflict might better be handled by others. One key is probably relationship. Who is in a position to best influence the responsible parties?

🛑 APPLY If a couple of leaders in your church were in conflict, what steps would you take?

_____

_____

_____

Of course, there would be no conflicts if every Christian adopted Jesus' attitude by making ourselves nothing. Problems usually occur when we consider ourselves somehow better than others—our opinions count for more, more behavior is more acceptable, or whatever.

Paul urged the Philippians to be *"blameless and innocent, children of God without blemish in the midst of a crooked and twisted generation, among whom you shine as lights in the world"* (Philippians 2:15).

Can we really be *"without blemish"*?

_____

_____

_____

_____

"Nobody's perfect"—a common phrase used to minimize all sorts of wrong behavior. In one sense, the saying is true. In Romans 3:23, Paul tells us, *"All have sinned and fall short of the glory of God."* On the other hand, Jesus tells us to *"be perfect, as your heavenly Father is perfect"* (Matthew 5:48). Would Jesus give people an impossible command? Paul agonized over this very dilemma.

📖 Read Romans 7:18–24.

Can you identify with Paul's lament? Do you sometimes feel as if there is part of you incapable of carrying out what you know you should do? Like Paul, have you cried out, "Who will deliver me?"

_____

_____

_____

_____

📖 Read Romans 7:24-25.

How can we be *"without blemish"*?

_____

_____

_____

_____

If you remain faithful to Christ, perpetually forgiven for your shortcomings, you can grow to perfection (completeness, maturity) through the Holy Spirit and in doing so, truly be a light to the world. That's my hope and my prayer. I hope it's also yours.

We'll never know—at least not in this lifetime—whether Euodia and Syntyche responded to Paul's plea or if the church carried them to Christ, restoring their light, but we can still attend to ourselves.

4

Epaphroditus
Suffering and Service

Among the obscure characters of the New Testament, barely known to most Christians, the name of Epaphroditus surely deserves our profound respect as one of the great models of ancient faith. When we read Paul's letter to the church in Philippi, a favorite of many Christians, do we gloss over the scant verses devoted to this man, eager to encounter the more famous theological nuggets from the pen of the apostle? To be sure, Philippians contains many scriptural gems, including the following verses as well as the ancient hymn preserved in 2:6–11.

"But our citizenship is in heaven, and from it we await a Savior, the Lord Jesus Christ." (3:20)

"Rejoice in the Lord always; again I will say, Rejoice." (4:4)

"And the peace of God, which surpasses all understanding, will guard your hearts and your minds in Christ Jesus." (4:7)

"Finally, brothers, whatever is true, whatever is honorable, whatever is just, whatever is pure, whatever is lovely, whatever is commendable, if there is any excellence, if there is anything worthy of praise, think about these things." (4:8)

"I can do all things through him who strengthens me." (4:13)

Put Yourself In Their Shoes
EPAPHRODITUS

Epaphroditus (*ep-af-ROD-ee-tos*) is a Greek from Philippi, whose name means "lovely."

Epaphroditus probably met Paul in AD 51 during the apostle's first missionary journey.

"My brother and fellow worker and fellow soldier, and your messenger and minister to me in my need." (Philippians 2:25)

The Philippian church heard of Paul's confinement, decided to send a monetary gift, and chose Epaphroditus to deliver it: *"I have received full payment, and more. I am well supplied, having received from Epaphroditus the gifts you sent, a fragrant offering, a sacrifice acceptable and pleasing to God"* (Philippians 4:18). This fact demonstrates the regard with which Epaphroditus was held by his own congregation. He may have been an elder of the church, a *diakonos* (deacon, servant), or perhaps simply a man recognized for his integrity and commitment.

Sometime during his journey or his stay with Paul, Epaphroditus became gravely ill and nearly died. News of his condition reached Philippi, and word of the church's grief had gotten back to Paul and Epaphroditus, causing Epaphroditus distress. Paul decided to send Epaphroditus back home and, together with Timothy (1:1), wrote a letter to this church that had been a faithful partner in the ministry of the gospel (1:5; 4:15). In it, he wrote of Epaphroditus: *"I have thought it necessary to send to you Epaphroditus my brother and fellow worker and fellow soldier, and your messenger and minister to my need"* (2:25).

In this single verse Paul applies five different highly significant labels to Epaphroditus, identifying him as one worthy of their honor (2:29). One of those labels, co-worker, is the unifying element of this series. We will look at the other four terms separately.

THE FAMILY OF GOD

Names for Followers of Jesus
"You shall leave your name to my chosen for a curse, and the Lord GOD will put you to death, but his servants he will call by another name." (Isaiah 65:15, emphasis added)

Just what is this other name Isaiah refers to? Throughout the gospels, followers of Jesus are usually referred to as disciples, but this term appears to have fallen largely out of use after the apostolic period (after the death of the last apostle in about AD 100). Traditionally, disciples were those who followed after a teacher and tried to emulate his life. After Jesus' death and resurrection, however, disciples could no longer follow Jesus in the traditional physical sense.

In the later New Testament (the letters of Paul, Peter, John, and others), the followers of Jesus were called by *many* names! In the chart that begins below, take a look at the passages where these names are used and explain the implications of each.

Name	Passage*	Implication
Soujourners/exiles	1 Peter 2:11	
Ambassador	2 Corinthians 5:20	
Heir	James 2:5	
Member	Ephesians 5:30	

Epaphroditus
DAY ONE

Word Study
WHO IS A SAINT

The term saint comes from the Greek word hagios, which according to Strong's Hebrew and Greek Dictionary means "sacred (physically pure, morally blameless or religious, ceremonially consecrated):—(most) holy (one, thing)." While some Christian traditions view saints as super-Christians who perform miracles, the biblical term applies to all Christians. If you are a Christian, you are a saint through the sacrifice of Jesus Christ.

Name	Passage*	Implication
Priest	1 Peter 2:11	
Saint	2 Corinthians 5:20	
Servant/minister	James 2:5	
Soldier	Ephesians 5:30	
Living stone	1 Peter 2:5	

* There are many additional instances of most of these labels. If you have a concordance, you may want to look up others.

The term *Christian* was not generally used in the apostolic church. In fact, *Christian* appears only three times in the New Testament and may have originally been used derisively by enemies of the church.

- *"In Antioch the disciples were first called Christians"* (Acts 11:26). Some people scoffed at Jesus' followers because He was crucified (a humiliating form of Roman execution). There are even instances of sarcastic inscriptions mocking adherence to a crucified man. For an opponent of the church, calling someone a Christian would be intended as an insult.

- During his imprisonment in Caesarea Maritima, Paul had an opportunity to present his testimony to Agrippa. The king replied, in what may well have been a sarcastic tone, *"In a short time would you persuade me to be a Christian?"* (Acts 26:28). There is no evidence that Agrippa ever did accept Christ, and it appears he was taunting Paul. Of course, Paul gladly accepted the name with typical irony: *"Whether short or long, I would to God that not only you but also all who hear me this day might become such as I am—except for these chains"* (Acts 26:29).

- In his first letter, intended for distribution to many churches, Peter wrote, *"Yet if anyone suffers as a Christian, let him not be ashamed, but let him glorify God in that name "* (1 Peter 4:16). Since the context is persecution, Peter was probably using the term the persecutors used. Like Paul, he turned the table on those seeking to belittle the church.

The Family of God

The fact that the term *Christian* may have originally been a kind of accusation does not imply there is anything wrong with it. Over the years, it lost the negative connotation, although there are certainly those today who used "Christian" derisively.

By far the most common term applied by early Christians to themselves, however, is *brother*. There are 185 instances of its use in the New Testament and an additional 33 uses of *children* (see, for example, 1 John 3:1).

The companion Greek terms *adelphos* (brother) and *adelphē* (sister) both derive from *delphus* (womb) and therefore mean a person or persons deriving from the same womb. The analogy of the church as a family is far and away the most common concept applied to the church in the New Testament, and it is important because it properly focuses the reality of the church on the people (rather than the focus of too many today on church as a building).

In one sense, all humans are brothers and sisters, owing our very existence to God, but Christians experience a special familial relationship. In calling Epaphroditus his brother, Paul is acknowledging him as a faithful member of the same family, each having been adopted by God as sons through Christ Jesus (see Romans 8:15; Galatians 4:4–5; Ephesians 1:5).

Christians are part of an *adelphotēs*, literally translated "brotherhood," but in the New Testament the term is used in reference to all who have been adopted into the family of God, without regard for gender. As such, the terms *adelphos* and *adelphē* carry with them a common hope, a common inheritance, and a common responsibility to serve as ambassadors through whom God is making his appeal to humanity (2 Corinthians 5:20).

Unfortunately, relationships in families are not always what they should be, but what does the family analogy tell us about God's expectations for interpersonal interactions within the church?

_____

_____

_____

APPLY What are the implications for interactions in our own families?

_____

_____

_____

_____

Epaphroditus

DAY TWO

SOLDIERS AND MESSENGERS

Soldiers

Paul used the term *soldier* to refer to Christians on four occasions in his letters. The first is in 1 Corinthians 9:7 where he replies to challenges to his apostleship and the financial support accompanying such a role. *"Who ever serves in the army at his own expense?"* he asks rhetorically.

📖 Read 1 Corinthians 9:1–7. What is Paul's point here?

_____

_____

_____

_____

Elsewhere Paul states that he has no need of support but wants to establish the right of an faithful evangelist to expect support from those he serves. He refers to both Epaphroditus (Philippians 2:25) and Philemon (Philemon 2) as his *"fellow soldiers."*

The final reference to Christians as soldiers comes in 2 Timothy 2:3–4, but before looking at the passage, jot down your thoughts about what it means to be a soldier.

_____

_____

_____

While it is true that the Christian life requires us to wage war against the forces of evil (see Ephesians 6:12), that battle is not primarily one of the violence and glory of military action.

📖 Now read 2 Timothy 2:3–4.

In what ways is the life of a good soldier one of self-sacrifice and hardship?

_____

_____

_____

_____

How had Epaphroditus exhibited the attributes of a good soldier?

_____

_____

_____

Messengers

When Paul refers to Epaphroditus as a messenger (*apostolos*), he is using the same word he applies to himself in the salutation of nine of his letters (Romans, 1 Corinthians, 2 Corinthians, Galatians, Ephesians, Colossians, 1 Timothy, 2 Timothy, and Titus). He claims his apostleship as a calling or *"by the will of God,"* citing his Damascus Road vision of the risen Christ as well as later revelations. Today, some make much of the distinction between *Apostles* and *apostles*, relegating anyone not among the original twelve (minus Judas Iscariot, plus Matthias, see Acts 1:16–26) to a lesser status. Paul's frequent defense of his own apostleship proves that even in his time there must have been those who insisted there could only be twelve apostles.

Yet in Scripture itself the descriptor *apostolos* is applied to people not among the Twelve. Take a look at each of these passages:

- 2 Corinthians 8:23
- Galatians 1:19
- Acts 14:14
- Hebrews 3:1

The literal meaning of *apostolos* is "one who is set apart and sent out (as a delegate or a commissioner)." An *apostolos* is sent to carry out the orders of the one who commissioned him or her. In some sense, every Christian could therefore be considered an *apostolos,* because all are set apart and sent out to spread the gospel (evangelize).

However, Paul strongly implies that not everyone is an apostle (1 Corinthians 12:29; Ephesians 4:11), so he must reserve the term for a special service. At the same time, *messenger* is probably a weak translation of *apostolos* since someone who merely carries a message need not have any particular stake in the message or broad commitment to the sender. So what is the difference between an *Apostle* and an *apostle*?

Who set apart Paul and the Twelve and sent them out?

_____

_____

_____

📖 Look at 2 Corinthians 12:12. How do the signs and wonders Paul refers to verify his apostleship? Why are they important?

_____

_____

_____

Signs and wonders were given to authoritative spokesmen for Christ in the early years of the church. These miraculous powers, delivered by God through the Holy Spirit, served as the certification of the bearer's authority.

Now take a look at these passages. In these cases, who commissioned and sent out the messenger?

- Acts 13:1–3 (Barnabas) _____
- 1 Corinthians 4:17 (Timothy) _____
- Ephesians 6:21–22 (Tychicus) _____
- Colossians 4:7–8 (Tychicus) _____
- Philippians 4:18 (Epaphroditus) _____

Does the fact that Paul and the Twelve were directly commissioned by God, while Barnabas, Tychicus, and Epaphroditus were commissioned by other Christians, make the message of one group more important than the other? Why or why not?

_____

_____

_____

_____

_____

What does the commission of Paul and the Twelve tell us about them?

_____

_____

_____

_____

What does the commission of Barnabas, Tychicus, and Epaphroditus tell us about them?

_____

_____

_____

APPLY Who has the responsibility to carry the gospel message to others?

_____

_____

SERVICE

In calling Epaphroditus a minister (*leitourgos*), Paul tells us that he provided service, fulfilling Paul's need. We do not know precisely what was involved in this service beyond the delivery of the gift from the church in Philippi, but we can assume at the least that Epaphroditus' presence comforted and encouraged Paul.

The more commonly used Greek word for *servant* or *minister* is *diakonos*, and service is a frequent theme of the New Testament. In human endeavors, we usually consider people to be successes if they are among the greatest in their fields of endeavor. A corporate executive is a success, a record-breaking athlete is a success, or a celebrated performer is a success. In biblical times, a learned Torah scholar was a success.

But Jesus presented a very different view of success.

📖 Read Mark 9:33–37.

How did the disciples' attitude mirror that prevalent in society both then and now?

_____

_____

_____

Most of us want and sometimes expect to be recognized for the things we do. In many social situations, success is measured by how far we have risen in an organization.

How does Jesus define success?

_____

_____

_____

To Jesus, the simplicity with which we accept Him and the humility we display in response represent success.

APPLY In this light, how can the children Jesus refers to in Matthew 18:3 be considered successful?

_____

_____

_____

_____

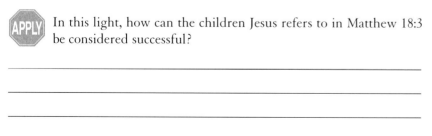

What does it mean to be a success in our culture? What does it mean to Jesus?

These children responded to Jesus without having to fully understand everything.

Paul refers to a number of people as *diakonos*. Look at the following passages and then respond to the questions.

📖 Read Romans 15:8–9; 16:1–2; 1 Corinthians 3:5; Ephesians 3:6–7; 6:21; Colossians 1:3–8; 1 Timothy 4:1–6.

What kind of service did Paul care about? That is, who or what were these people servants of?

_____

_____

_____

There is service to those who do not know Christ Jesus, and there is also service within the church.

📖 Read Ephesians 4:11–13.

What is the goal of service to brothers and sisters within the church?

_____

_____

_____

The goal of service to other Christians is to help everyone—both the giver and the receiver—attain maturity so that we may fully appreciate God's gifts.

Paul's use of the term *leitourgos*, as opposed to *diakonos*, in his commendation of Epaphroditus is unusual. He uses *leitourgos* in only two other instances: in Romans 15:15–16 he applies *leiturgos* to himself, and in Romans 13:6 he calls human rulers *leitourgos* of God.

This last use more reflects the literal meaning of *leiturgos*, which is derived from *laos* (people) and *ergon* (work)—the peoples' work, or public service. Consequently, Epaphroditus's *leitourgos* is related to his *apostolos*, in that he faithfully carried out his mission as a public servant of the *ekklesia* in Philippi. Paul therefore gives Epaphroditus double praise, affirming that the Philippians' commission of him was well done.

Epaphroditus

DAY FOUR

SUFFERING

"[Epaphroditus] has been longing for you all and has been distressed because you heard that he was ill. Indeed he was ill, near to death. But God had mercy on him, and not only on him but on me also, lest I should have sorrow upon sorrow. I am the more eager to send him, therefore, that you may rejoice at seeing him again, and that I may be less anxious. So receive him in the Lord with all joy, and honor such men, for he nearly died for the work of Christ, risking his life to complete what was lacking in your service to me."
(Philippians 2:26–30)

The question that begs to be asked is, "Why didn't Paul heal Epaphroditus?" There are several possibilities:

- Perhaps he did. Paul certainly had the gift of healing. He healed the crippled man in Lystra (Acts 14:8–10). He banished an unclean spirit from the divining slave girl in Philippi (Acts 16:16–18). In Ephesus, even pieces of cloth he had touched had curative powers (Acts 19:11–12). On Malta, he healed the father of the island's leading man (Acts 28:8–9). The text of Philippians does not tell us how Epaphroditus recovered, only that he did. Perhaps Paul healed him and simply didn't say so because he did not want to focus on himself, but the context does not seem to support this interpretation.

- Perhaps Epaphroditus had already recovered by the time he reached Rome (or Ephesus), but Paul seems to have observed Epaphroditus's illness firsthand.

- Paul chose not to heal him or, more precisely, God chose not to heal him miraculously. Every instance of healing in the New Testament is clearly attributed to God. The human healers were only instruments of God's will.

Take a look at the story of Peter and John healing the man lame from birth in Acts 3:1–13. There are always many people afflicted with a variety of diseases and conditions. God does not heal them all, nor is there any evidence that the apostles healed all the sick in Jerusalem.

APPLY What was the purpose of healing *this* man?

_____

_____

_____

The purpose of all New Testament healings was to display the power of God so that people might believe.

📖 Now read 1 Corinthians 12:4–11.

What role do people have in the acquisition of miraculous gifts?

_____

_____

_____

People have no role whatsoever in the acquisition of miraculous gifts. They are apportioned as God sees fit to serve His purposes.

APPLY What role do people play in the display of miraculous gifts?

_____

_____

_____

People are expected to boldly display the gifts God bestows. What is the purpose of miraculous gifts?

_____

_____

The purpose of miraculous gifts in the early church was to serve the common good in order to display God's power.

Would Paul's healing Epaphroditus serve this purpose?

_____

_____

A miraculous healing of Epaphroditus probably would not have served a compelling purpose. In this case, his natural recovery, accompanied by suffering, may have better served God's purposes.

Paul certainly empathized with Epaphroditus's suffering, since Paul himself was apparently physically weak (2 Corinthians 10:10) and he attests to being *"often near death"* during his ministry (see 2 Corinthians 11:23–27). But Paul had learned the value of weakness, whether through suffering or personal shortcomings.

📖 Read 1 Corinthians 1:26–31.
What is a value of weakness?

_____

_____

_____

When people accomplish things they could not on their own (in their weakness), the power of God is displayed.

Appropriately, Paul's most powerful testimony of his own weakness comes immediately after his description of an event in which he might be justifiably proud. Forced to defend his apostleship and his ministry against detractors, Paul reveals a sublime mystical experience—a vision of the third heaven. Read 2 Corinthians 12:1–4.

Paul goes on to tell how God counterbalanced this experience.

📖 Read 2 Corinthians 12:5–9.
What was Paul's first reaction to this *"thorn . . . in the flesh"*?

_____

_____

_____

Just as most of us would, Paul wanted to be relieved of this problem.

Did God answer Paul's prayers?

_____

_____

_____

Paul seems to think so. He understood the lesson God taught him and shared the insight with the Corinthians: *"For the sake of Christ, then, I am content with weaknesses, insults, hardships, persecutions, and calamities. For when I am weak, then I am strong"* (2 Corinthians 12:10).

Regardless of the severity of Epaphroditus's illness, his spirit must have soared when Paul related that wisdom—the Philippian had traveled in loving Christian service to bring a gift to a prisoner. When he became weak for the sake of Christ, he became strong. In their respective suffering, Paul and Epaphroditus came to identify even more closely with Christ Jesus who, as Paul writes, *"was crucified in weakness"* (2 Corinthians 13:4).

How Can I Serve?

Epaphroditus

DAY FIVE

Epaphroditus, although obscure in Christian history, provides one of the Bible's greatest lessons on serving. Despite weakness and suffering from a near-fatal illness, he fulfilled his service to Paul on behalf of his Philippian brothers and sisters and on behalf of God. In doing so, he became a powerful source of encouragement for the man who, more than anyone other than Jesus, spread God's message to the world.

The lesson the brief story of Epaphroditus teaches us about God is profound: **what matters to God is more the manner in which we serve rather than the size of the service.**

Several months after Hurricane Katrina hit the Gulf Coast, I joined a group composed mostly of college students "mucking out" houses in devastated St. Bernard Parish. By the middle of the first day, I knew there was no way I could continue the work. At fifty six, I simply didn't have the strength and stamina of the young men and women around me. The thought crossed my mind to ask for one of the easier jobs—cooking for the team or working in a relief-supply warehouse. Under most circumstances, I would have succumbed to my own weakness.

Instead, I asked God to give me strength in my weakness, and He answered my prayer, allowing me to be a source of encouragement to the others. For one of few times in my life, I knew that I had let God use me.

APPLY Have you ever experienced a time when you were weak—sick or tired—and someone asked you to do something for them? How did you respond?

_____

_____

_____

_____

Have you ever received service from someone whom you realized (perhaps later) was suffering in some way? How did you feel about that person?

_____

_____

_____

_____

LESSON FOUR – EPAPHRODITUS   51

Think about a time you provided some service when you really didn't feel like doing so. What did the other person get out of this?

_____

_____

_____

What did you get out of this?

_____

_____

_____

What are the service opportunities around you now that you consider beyond your capacity?

_____

_____

_____

In what ways might God be glorified if you overcame your own weaknesses and served others in these ways?

_____

_____

_____

Surely one of the most challenging concepts in Christianity—and one which is contrary to human wisdom—is the value of suffering. *"For the sake of Christ, then, I am content with weaknesses, insults, hardships, persecutions, and calamities. For when I am weak, then I am strong."* (James 1:2).

It's one thing to advocate tolerating suffering; it's quite another to suggest that suffering should be a source of joy. There are those who suggest that suffering is the supreme service, but that misses the point. Suffering in and of itself has no intrinsic value. Stoic philosophy, somewhat popular in upper Roman classes during the early years of the church, taught that suffering was to be endured and overcome. "If you are distressed by any external thing," Marcus Aurelius (AD 121–180) wrote, "it is not this thing which disturbs you, but your own judgment about it. And it is in your power to wipe out that judgment now" (*Meditations*, 8.49)—the ancient equivalent of "Get over it!"

In Christianity, however, the value of suffering lies not in getting over it but in allowing God to use it to strengthen His followers. *"(F)or you know that the testing of your faith produces steadfastness,"* James explains (1:3). The fruit of suffering comes when we place complete trust in God, confident that His purposes will produce a positive outcome, even if it's not one the sufferer will ever see.

Similarly, there are those today who claim the gospel is about wealth and prosperity, a skewed version of Jesus' words in John 10:10 (*"I came that they may have life and have it abundantly,"*), apparently forgetting that Jesus also said, *"One's life does not consist in the abundance of his possessions"* (Luke

In Christianity, the value of suffering lies not in getting over it but in allowing God to use it to strengthen His followers.

12:15). The abundance of life Christ Jesus offers lies neither in wealth and prosperity nor in suffering, but rather in every aspect of life and the glory we give to God regardless of the circumstance.

Paul wrote precisely this near the end of his letter to the church in Philippi: *"I know how to be brought low, and I know how to abound. In any and every circumstance, I have learned the secret of facing plenty and hunger, abundance and need. I can do all things through him who strengthens me"* (Philippians 4:12–13). When Epaphroditus returned to Philippi, perhaps he read Paul's letter aloud to the assembled Christians. When he read those words, he must have smiled and nodded.

APPLY What can you do to be an Epaphroditus to someone today?

_____

_____

_____

What's holding you back?

_____

_____

_____

If you're missing service opportunities—whether sharing the gospel with those who do not know Jesus or building up your brothers and sisters or simply easing someone else's burdens—because of your weakness, ask God to carry you through it.

5

Demas
Conflicting Priorities

Among the letters Paul wrote to churches while under house arrest in Rome are two he sent to Colossae—one to the church as a whole and the other to Philemon, a church leader. (In this lesson I assume Paul wrote the Colossian letters from Rome.) In each, he added greetings from several of his companions, including one named Demas (Colossians 4:14; Philemon 1:24). In the more personal letter to Philemon, he referred to Demas as his fellow worker (*sunergos sunergos*). This is not a label Paul threw around casually, seemingly reserving it for his closest companions.

It is not likely that Paul would include greetings from someone who did not share his commitment to Christ and to spreading the gospel. Furthermore, Luke reports that only he and Aristarchus were with the apostle when Paul left Jerusalem under guard to be transported by ship to Rome (Acts 27:2), so we can conclude that Demas, who seems to have been a Thessalonian, had heard about Paul's confinement and traveled to the capital, as others did, to be with him—no small commitment in those days. Paul may have been confident of his release, but just being a Christian in Rome represented considerable risk. From this evidence we can be very confident that at the time Paul wrote Colossians and Philemon, Demas was his close associate and a faithful Christian.

Put Yourself In Their Shoes
DEMAS

Demas (*day-MAS*) was probably a Thessalonia Greek, whose name means "governor of the people."

Demas probably met Paul in AD 51 during the apostle's first missionary journey.

"Epaphras, my fellow prisoner in Christ Jesus, sends greetings to you, and so do Mark, Aristarchus, Demas, and Luke, my fellow workers." (Philemon 23–24)

It comes as a major disappointment, therefore, when Paul reports to Timothy just three or four years later, that *"Demas, in love with this present world, has deserted me and gone to Thessalonica"* (2 Timothy 4:10). Why did Demas, honored as a co-worker and apparently risking everything to be near Paul, later desert him? The answer seems simple: he was *"in love with this present world,"* according to Paul, but just what does that mean?

LIVING UP TO PAUL

"*For Demas, in love with this present world, has deserted me and gone to Thessalonica*" (2 Timothy 4:10). Poor Demas! With these fifteen words (thirteen in Greek), Demas became fodder for countless sermons on everything from lack of commitment to apostasy.

Several biblical figures learned it wasn't always easy to be around Paul. He could at times be harsh, sarcastic, judgmental, and dismissive. Once a Pharisee and the merciless persecutor of the church, his encounter with the risen Jesus did not change his innately passionate personality—he merely changed sides. Just as no Judean Christian was safe from his zeal, so too no timid or hypocritical Christian escaped his judgment. He was effusive in praise and venomous in condemnation. To understand the standard Demas had to uphold, let's look at a few examples of Paul's interactions with others, beginning with no less than Peter.

📖 Read Galatians 2:11–14.

What strong charges does Paul levy against Peter?

_____

_____

_____

We can certainly applaud Paul for his defense of Gentile Christians, but calling Jesus' arguably closest disciple condemned and guilty of hypocrisy in a public letter seems a bit excessive to me. Of course, he did it the right way, opposing Peter to his face instead of gossiping behind his back as others might.

📖 Read Galatians 3:1–3.

What does Paul call the Galatians?

_____

_____

_____

📖 Read Matthew 5:22.

Was Paul guilty of precisely what Jesus condemned?

_____

_____

_____

Certainly, Paul needed to counter the false, Judaizing teacher influencing the Galatians, and perhaps his anger was exactly what the Galatians needed, but we have to wonder if every Galatian was receptive to his message after being called foolish.

📖 Read Acts 13:1–5, 13; 15:35–40.

What do you think of Paul's rejection of John Mark and his disagreement with Barnabas?

_____

_____

_____

To me at least, this is not one of Paul's shining moments. While his reservations about John Mark may be justified, it is difficult to understand how he could part with such a trusted co-worker as Barnabas over the disagreement. After all, Barnabas was the individual who testified on Paul's behalf to Jesus' apostles (Acts 9:27–28) and later traveled to Tarsus and brought him to Antioch (Acts 11:25–26).

On the other hand, there are nearly countless examples of Paul displaying patience with others, and ultimately he was hardest on himself.

📖 Read, for example, Romans 7:15–24.

Paul was a very complex, passionate man, and when we study his comments about Demas, we need to understand his occasional severity.

Falling Away

"*For Demas, in love with this present world, has deserted me and gone to Thessalonica*" (2 Timothy 4:10).

Does Paul's statement indicate that Demas turned his back on Christ and rejected the Christian faith?

_____

_____

_____

I don't think so. If Demas had rejected Christ, Paul undoubtedly would have said so, being the kind of person he was. He was not bashful in naming some who had rejected Christ. See, for example, 1 Timothy 1:19–20. Paul's prescription for Hymenaeus and Alexander is that they be "*handed over to Satan.*" What does this mean?

_____

_____

_____

Paul used the same phrase in the first letter to the church in Corinth.

Demas

🔍 *Did You Know?*

❓ **ANCIENT CON-DEMNATION**

While Demas gets little love from modern commentators and preachers, his harshest critic was probably a fourth century church leader named Epiphanius (about AD 315–403), who placed Paul's former co-worker alongside Ebion and Cerinthus as one of the foremost heretics of the early church. Epiphanius, however, may have been referring to the characterization of Demas in the apocryphal Acts of Paul and Thecla, where he is an envious hypocrite who turns on Paul for money. There is simply no genuine basis for Epiphanius's treatment of Demas.

📖 Read 1 Corinthians 5:1–13.

Why does Paul command the Corinthians to expel the incestuous man from the church?

_____

_____

_____

Expulsion from the church is an extreme measure because it cuts someone off from the blessings God bestows on His people. In the case of Hymenaeus, Alexander, and the Corinthian, the action was presumably preceded by multiple attempts to correct and warn them. But these having failed, Paul was concerned about both the congregation and the persistent sinner.

What does Paul mean by *"a little leaven leavens the whole lump"* (1 Corinthians 5:6)?

_____

_____

_____

Paul had a twofold concern about keeping unrepentant sinners in a congregation. One was the potential negative effect on the other members (leavening the whole lump). What was the other?

_____

_____

_____

Paul's purpose in turning someone over to Satan was not simply to protect others; he also hoped the shame the expelled member experienced would lead to repentance. In a society where honor and shame mattered, being cut off from friends could have a sobering effect.

APPLY Do you think expulsion from the church is still an effective tactic today? Why or why not?

_____

_____

_____

Some commentators have suggested the name Demas is a contraction of Demetrius and that Paul's Demas is the same person as Demetrius in 3 John 1:12, whom John says *"received a good testimony from everyone, and from the truth itself."* John went on, *"We also add our testimony, and you know that our testimony is true."*

John's comment (written from Ephesus) seems to refer to someone about whom there was some question, and Paul's letter was written to Timothy in Ephesus. If somehow Demas had made his way to Asia, and people there were familiar with Paul's comment, it would make sense for John to update the information about Demas. That conclusion, however, is pure conjecture, and placing Demas in Ephesus is a stretch. Unfortunately, we don't know what Demas did after he deserted Paul and returned to Thessalonica.

WORLDLY CONCERNS

One of the two most common interpretations of *"in love with this present world"* is that Demas left Paul to deal with some business or family matter. In his classic commentary, Matthew Henry (1662–1714) wrote that Demas may have been "called off from his ministry by secular affairs, in which he entangled himself; his first love to Christ and his gospel was forsaken and forgotten, and he fell in love with the world."

This may be, because the Greek phrase *nun aiōn*, usually translated "present world," literally means "now age," suggesting Demas may have been more interested in the here and now than in the future or eternity. In this argument, Demas became more interested in some pressing secular issue than in spreading the good news. Sound familiar? How many of us let the busyness of life divert us from our primary purpose as Christians?

Can you present any evidence that this conclusion about Demas is unlikely?

_____

_____

_____

To answer that question, let's look at what we know about Demas, which is admittedly very little. Luke mentions him nowhere in Acts, so we do not know when and how he became associated with Paul. Other than the 2 Timothy passage about his desertion of Paul, Demas is mentioned only twice:

"Luke the beloved physician greets you, as does Demas" (Colossians 4:14).

"Epaphras, my fellow prisoner in Christ Jesus, sends greetings to you, and so do Mark, Aristarchus, Demas, and Luke, my fellow workers" (Philemon 23–24).

Both Colossians and Philemon are generally believed to have been written during Paul's first Roman imprisonment (about AD 60–62). In both cases, Paul ends the letter, as he often did, with personal greetings from his companions. At this time, Demas is with Paul in Rome, and Paul refers to him as a fellow worker (co-worker).

If Colossians and Philemon were written during Paul's first imprisonment in Rome, and 2 Timothy was written at least four years later during Paul's second imprisonment, what does this suggest about Demas?

_____

_____

_____

_____

Many biblical scholars believe Paul made a fifth missionary journey between his two Roman imprisonments (see the Titus lesson in this study), perhaps to Spain. While it's possible Demas went somewhere else during that time, the most reasonable assumption is that he was with Paul. If so, it seems rather doubtful some pressing business concern would suddenly call him away. On the other hand, if Demas's departure was prompted by a business matter, Paul's comment seems justified.

📖 Read Matthew 6:24.

What does this passage mean to you? Is it wrong for a Christian to have a secular job?

_____

_____

_____

Paul addressed this issue.

📖 Read 2 Thessalonians 3:10–12.

What is Paul's attitude toward those who do not earn their own living?

_____

_____

_____

Apparently some Thessalonica Christians stopped working for a living and expected the church to support them. Paul is unequivocal, commanding them to earn their own living. While it's possible Demas let business distract him from his mission as Paul's co-worker, it simply doesn't seem likely. If not a business matter, what about a family emergency?

📖 Read Luke 14:26.

How do you interpret this passage? Does Jesus expect His followers to unequivocally turn their backs on their families?

_____

_____

_____

Jesus uses hyperbole in this passage, and it is better understood in the parallel passage in Matthew (10:37), where Jesus comments on those who love their families more than Him. When we put *anyone*, including our closest relatives or friends, ahead of Christ, we have a problem!

Paul also commented on relationships with family.

📖 Read 1 Timothy 5:8.

Would Paul disapprove of Demas leaving him to deal with an important family matter?

_____

_____

_____

It certainly doesn't seem so. Paul lamented those who turned their backs on him (see also 2 Timothy 1:15), but he would never be so uncharitable as to lambast someone taking care of their own family.

Doctrine

HYPERBOLIC LANGUAGE

Luke 14:26 is a favorite verse of cynics who deny Christ and attack Christianity. "There, Jesus is a misogynist!" they claim, but they insist on a literal reading that ignores the cultural context. Such extreme language was and is common among Semitic cultures and is frequently found in ancient texts, including the Bible. Another example is found in Matthew 6:24. What these two passages really mean is that a disciple of Jesus must be prepared to correct or walk away from any job or relationship threatening his or her relationship with God.

FEAR OF PERSECUTION

J esus told His disciples, *"If they persecuted me, they will also persecute you"* (John 15:20), and history bears testimony to extensive persecution of Christians. It began in the earliest days of the church. Jews, incensed at the "blasphemy" of calling Jesus God, routinely attacked the church. Paul says he attempted to destroy the church (Galatians 1:13). After his conversion, he was nearly stoned to death in Lystra during his first mission trip (Acts 14:19).

Another famous incident occurred in Ephesus during Paul's third missionary journey.

📖 Read about the riot of the silversmiths in Acts 19:23–41.

What specific details about this incident reveal the genuine danger involved?

_____

_____

_____

When angry mobs gather, bad things tend to happen, and Paul's friends had to dissuade him from going to the theater. The town clerk obviously recognized how charged the atmosphere was, and the primary duty of Roman provincial officials was to keep peace. Nothing would get them removed from their lucrative positions quicker than unrest among the populace.

Fear is a natural and reasonable response to a threat. Certainly Aristarchus and Gaius must have feared for their lives in Ephesus. Would Demas have had reason to fear for his life in Rome? The answer is a resounding yes!

In AD 64 a fire devastated much of Rome, and in its aftermath rumors circulated that Emperor Nero had ordered the burning of part of the city so that he could rebuild it according to his notions of urban development. To divert attention from himself, he needed a scapegoat. Read the following passage written by the Roman historian Cornelius Tacitus:

> Consequently, to get rid of the report, Nero fastened the guilt and inflicted the most exquisite tortures on a class hated for their abominations, called Christians by the populace. Christus, from whom the name had its origin, suffered the extreme penalty during the reign of Tiberius at the hands of one of our procurators, Pontius Pilatus, and a most mischievous superstition, thus checked for the moment, again broke out not only in Judaea, the first source of the evil, but even in Rome, where all things hideous and shameful from every part of the world find their centre and become popular. Accordingly, an arrest was first made of all who pleaded guilty; then, upon their information, an immense multitude was convicted, not so much of the crime of firing the city, as of hatred against mankind. Mockery of every sort was added to their deaths. Covered with the skins of beasts, they were torn by dogs and perished, or were nailed to crosses, or were doomed to the flames and burnt, to serve as a nightly illumination, when daylight had expired. Nero offered his gardens for the spectacle, and was exhibiting a show in

Did You Know?

ROMAN VIEWS OF CHRISTIANITY

Tacitus wasn't the only Roman historian to attest to Nero's persecution of Christians. In an almost parenthetical note, Gaius Suetonius Tranquillus, another second-century writer, commented, "Punishment by Nero was inflicted on the Christians, a class of men given to a new and mischievous superstition" (*Lives of the Caesars: Nero,* 16.2). Romans considered Christians antisocial atheists because they did not participate in Roman holiday festivities or worship traditional Roman gods. In addition, because of misunderstandings about the Lord's Supper, rumors circulated that Christians practiced human sacrifice and cannibalism. Some also thought Christians to be incestuous because of the calls to brotherly love.

the circus, while he mingled with the people in the dress of a charioteer or stood aloft on a car. Hence, even for criminals who deserved extreme and exemplary punishment, there arose a feeling of compassion; for it was not, as it seemed, for the public good, but to glut one man's cruelty, that they were being destroyed. (*Annals*, 15.44)

What pervasive attitude about Christians is revealed in Tacitus's comments?

_____

_____

_____

Tacitus refers to Christianity as a mischievous superstition, hideous and shameful, and to Christians as criminals deserving of extreme punishment. I get the impression of a witch hunt in Rome, with people whipped into a frenzy by claims that Christians were responsible for the destruction of their city. Can any of us say we would not be terrified in such an environment?

📖 Read Matthew 10:23.

Does this passage relate to Demas?

_____

_____

_____

In the second and third centuries, martyrdom became a popular phenomenon, if we can consider death popular. Until Emperor Constantine converted to Christianity in AD 312, Christians endured sporadic persecutions by imperial and provincial officials, and martyrdom came to be seen as the ultimate expression of faith because it represented a re-creation of the death of Jesus.

The most well-known biblical martyrdom is that of Stephen, one of the men chosen by the apostles to tend to routine matters (Acts 6:1–6).

📖 Read Acts 6:9–7:60 and the following excerpt from *The Martyrdom of Polycarp*. (Polycarp was a leader of the church in Smyrna who was executed in about AD 155.)

When he had pronounced this amen, and so finished his prayer, those who were appointed for the purpose kindled the fire. And as the flame blazed forth in great fury, we, to whom it was given to witness it, beheld a great miracle, and have been preserved that we might report to others what then took place. For the fire, shaping itself into the form of an arch, like the sail of a ship when filled with the wind, encompassed as by a circle the body of the martyr. And he appeared within not like flesh which is burnt, but as bread that is baked, or as gold and silver glowing in a furnace. Moreover, we perceived such a sweet odour [coming from the pile], as if frankincense or some such precious spices had been smoking there. (*The Martyrdom of Polycarp*, 15)

How are the accounts of Stephen and Polycarp alike?

_____

_____

_____

How are they different?

_____

_____

In the second and third centuries, martyrdom stories were the best sellers of Christian literature. They became highly stylized, invariably including fantastic feats of endurance. They were collected into volumes and read publicly in churches. Martyrdom became so much a fabric of Christianity that some people actively sought the opportunity to die for Christ. In an era of sometimes intense persecution, such stories served to inspire the Christian community, but not everyone was enamored with martyrdom. The writer of the recently translated *Gospel of Judas*, for example, excoriated the mainstream church for its glorification of martyrdom, claiming it represented an inappropriate return to the Mosaic sacrificial system.

📖 Read Romans 14:7–9.

What attitude do you think Paul would have toward someone who deliberately sought martyrdom?

_____

_____

_____

WHAT ARE MY PRIORITIES?

If Paul's comment *"in love with this present world"* means that Demas didn't want to die, there is at least one other biblical figure who would, on perhaps two occasions, merit the same accusation. Almost everyone is familiar with Peter's three denials of Jesus on the night He was arrested, but a less well-known story from the apocryphal *Acts of Peter* suggests he again attempted to avoid trouble years later.

According to the story, Peter was in Rome during the Neronian persecutions, and friends convinced him to flee from the capital when his life seemed threatened. On the road out of Rome, Peter encountered Jesus (perhaps in a vision) and asked Him, "Where are you going, Lord?" (Latin *Quo vadis, Domine*). When Jesus answered that He was going to Rome to be crucified again, Peter returned to the city where, according to legend, he was crucified upside down.

 In the West, we do not risk physical harm or death for practicing Christianity—persecution is much more subtle. Are there costs in our society for being a Christian? If so, what are some of them?

_____

_____

_____

Years ago, when I worked for a major school publisher, I attended a meeting with several high-ranking company officials, discussing the future of

Word Study

MARTUS

The word *martyrdom* comes from the Greek word *martus*, which means "a witness" and is used by Paul in reference to Stephen in Acts 22:20. Courage in the face of torture or death served as a powerful witness of people's faith in Christ Jesus. Roman officials were baffled by Christians. When they executed leaders of other undesirable groups, those groups fell apart. When they executed Christian leaders, Christianity grew.

Demas

DAY FIVE

Word Study

APOCRYPHAL

The word *apocryphal* comes from the Greek word for "hidden" and refers to books written about Jesus and His disciples that are not included in our New Testament. Some of these books are merely fiction filling in gaps in the canon, such as the *Infancy Gospel of James*, which portrays Jesus as a child. Others, like the *Acts of Andrew*, portray the fantastical exploits of the apostles. Still others, like the *Gospel of the Savior*, present very different views of Jesus and Christianity than those in the New Testament. In contrast to skeptical claims like those presented in *The Da Vinci Code*, decisions about which books did and did not belong in an official collection was not made by any individual or church council. Rather, the canon developed gradually and organically, as works were accepted by the many churches around the Mediterranean world.

public school textbooks and testing. One of the officials commented about the influence of "wacko Christian fundamentalists." I remained silent at the time, fearful that speaking out would destroy any credibility I might have with the group.

APPLY What opportunities have you had in your life when you could have spoken out for Jesus and failed to do so?

_____

_____

_____

_____

What if you had it to do over again? Would you act differently? Why or why not?

_____

_____

_____

As I discussed earlier, some commentators believe Demas deserted Paul to attend to some personal business or family issue. Have you ever let such issues distract you from serving God? When and why?

_____

_____

_____

_____

If you set Christian service as the top priority, what would change in your life?

_____

_____

_____

_____

How do you think Christians should establish their priorities?

_____

_____

_____

_____

Personally, I don't think all Christians are called to act in all circumstances. Paul tells us gifts of the Holy Spirit are apportioned to each Christian as God wills (1 Corinthians 12:4–11). We have different measures of faith, wisdom, and knowledge. In addition, we have different levels of maturity. We have a problem, however, if we use this concept as an excuse ("That's not my gift") and do nothing. As Christians, we need to respond to the opportunities presented to each of us.

6

Titus
A Trustworthy Partner

As I studied Paul's co-workers for this book, I was consistently amazed. By every indication, these were very ordinary people before their encounters with the gospel. Not all of them are heroic, but often they sacrificed everything to help Paul spread the message. I am amazed by the loyalty of Aristarchus, the commitment of Epaphroditus, and boldness of Prisca and Aquila. This chapter looks at yet another amazing individual, known by most Christians only through the letter Paul wrote to him. Inexplicably, and despite what may have been an association with Paul of as much as twenty years, Titus is not mentioned once in **Acts**. We know nothing of his life before he became a Christian, but from Paul's letters we can reconstruct key elements of his new life.

Put Yourself In Their Shoes
TITUS

Titus (*TEE-tos*)—"nurse"

In the words of Paul:

"As for Titus, he is my partner and fellow worker for your benefit. And as for our brothers, they are messengers of the churches, the glory of Christ." (2 Corinthians 8:23)

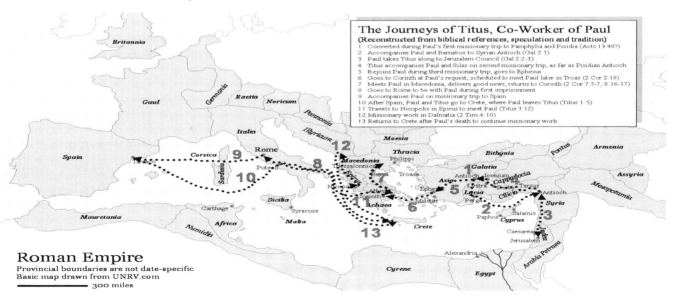

The Journeys of Titus, Co-Worker of Paul
(Reconstructed from biblical references, speculation and tradition)
1 Converted during Paul's first missionary trip to Pamphylia and Pisidia (Acts 13:48?)
2 Accompanies Paul and Barnabus to Syrian Antioch (Gal 2:1)
3 Paul takes Titus along to Jerusalem Council (Gal 2:2-3)
4 Titus accompanies Paul and Silas on second missionary trip, as far as Pisidian Antioch
5 Rejoins Paul during third missionary trip, goes to Ephesus
6 Goes to Corinth at Paul's request, scheduled to meet Paul later in Troas (2 Cor 2:18)
7 Meets Paul in Macedonia, delivers good news, returns to Corinth (2 Cor 7:5-7, 8:16-17)
8 Goes to Rome to be with Paul during first imprisonment
9 Accompanies Paul on missionary trip to Spain
10 After Spain, Paul and Titus go to Crete, where Paul leaves Titus (Titus 1:5)
11 Travels to Nicopolis in Epirus to meet Paul (Titus 3:12)
12 Missionary work in Dalmatia (2 Tim 4:10)
13 Returns to Crete after Paul's death to continue missionary work

Roman Empire
Provincial boundaries are not date-specific
Basic map drawn from UNRV.com
— 300 miles

CONVERSION

Chronologically, the first mention of Titus comes in Galatians 2:1–3, where Paul reports that he took Titus along with him to the so-called Jerusalem Council in AD 49, but we can surmise something about Titus's conversion. In his letter to Titus, Paul refers to him as *"my true child"* (Titus 1:4), a label he applied to only two others—Timothy (1 Corinthians 4:17; 1 Timothy 1:2, 18; 2 Timothy 1:2; 2:1) and Onesimus (Philemon 1:10).

What might make Timothy, Onesimus, and Titus "true children" of Paul?

_____

_____

_____

"My true child" probably indicates they were converted directly through the ministry of Paul. In all likelihood, Titus first heard the gospel from Paul and was baptized (reborn) into Christ by him, making Paul his spiritual "father."

Where this occurred is uncertain, but a clue may lie in the fact that Paul chose to bring Titus with him to Jerusalem. In the early church, one of the major controversies involved Jewish law, particularly circumcision, which was the external sign God gave to Abraham for His chosen people. After Paul returned from his first missionary journey (AD 47–48), the controversy broke out in Antioch:

> *"But some men came down from Judea and were teaching the brothers, 'Unless you are circumcised according to the custom of Moses, you cannot be saved.' And after Paul and Barnabas had no small dissension and debate with them, Paul and Barnabas and some of the others were appointed to go up to Jerusalem to the apostles and the elders about this question."* (Acts 15:1–2)

While a thorough investigation of the relationship between law and grace is far beyond the scope of this study, it is helpful at this point to know something about Paul's attitude. Some argued adherence to the law was a prerequisite to becoming a Christian. Look up the following verses and fill in the blanks.

Romans 6:14. *"For ___SIN___ will have no dominion over you, since you are not under ___LAW___ but under ___GRACE___ ."*

Romans 7:6. *"But now we are released from the ___LAW___, having died to that which held us captive, so that we serve not under the old written ___LAW___ but in the _____ ___NEWNESS___ of the ___SPIRIT___."*

Galatians 5:18. *"But if you are led by the ___SPIRIT___, you are not under the ___LAW___ ."*

As a teacher, the law revealed sin by revealing divine concepts of right and wrong, but now, Paul argues, Christians are controlled by the Spirit rather than law.

Back to Titus. Luke reports simply that the Antioch church appointed *"Paul and Barnabas and some of the others"* to meet with the apostles and elders in Jerusalem (Acts 15:2). In Paul's own account of the trip to Jerusalem, however, he reports he took Titus along (Galatians 2:1).

📖 Read both Paul's (Galatians 2:1–10) and Luke's (Acts 15:1–30) accounts of the Jerusalem Council and answer the following questions.

Besides the specific issue of the law and particularly circumcision, what seems to have been at stake for Paul in Jerusalem?

_____

_____

_____

Paul's entire ministry may have been under some attack. Stories had filtered back to the Jewish Christians in Jerusalem, and some were certainly horrified by his message that Gentiles need not adhere to the Mosaic law to be Christians.

What were the results of the council?

_____

_____

_____

_____

What role do you think Titus played in this event?

_____

_____

_____

_____

Ultimately, what was at stake involved the entire future of Christianity in the Roman world. Most Romans considered the Jewish practice of circumcision nothing less than barbarism. Had it become a prerequisite to Christian baptism, it would have presented a substantial obstacle to the Gentiles Paul sought to reach with the gospel of freedom. Peter's words— *"Why are you putting God to the test by placing a yoke on the neck of the disciples that neither our fathers nor we have been able to bear?"* (Acts 15:10)—seem to have been the pivotal moment.

At the same time, Titus was probably exhibit A in Paul's presentation to the Jerusalem church. Here was a full-blooded Greek Christian who had heard and responded to Paul's preaching. That he was apparently willing to travel to Antioch and then on to Jerusalem with Paul surely served as a demonstration of his enthusiasm for the gospel. His faith may well have been a contributing factor to the decision that the Mosaic law did not apply to Gentile Christians.

Of course, the Jerusalem Council did not end the attempts by some to enforce Mosaic law. Most of Paul's Galatian letter seeks to counter the Judaizers' apparently somewhat successful teaching in Galatia.

Word Study
THE PURPOSE OF THE LAW

Depending on your Bible translation, Galatians 3:24 may describe the law as a *"guardian"* (ESV), *"tutor"* (NASB), *"schoolmaster"* (KJV), *"teacher"* (CEV), or one *"put in charge"* (NIV). The Greek word is *paidagōgos*. According to *Thayer's Greek Definitions*, a *paidagōgos* in Greek and Roman society was a "trustworthy slave who were charged with the duty of supervising the life and morals of boys belonging to the better class. The boys were not allowed so much as to step out of the house without them before arriving at the age of manhood." Paul implies that the law served a similar purpose to the immature children of Abraham until God's plan reached completion in Christ Jesus.

WHERE DID TITUS BECOME A CHRISTIAN?

Titus was almost certainly converted during Paul's first mission trip to Cyprus, Pisidian Antioch, Iconium, Lystra, and Derbe. When Paul entered a new city for the first time, his consistent strategy was to go first to the synagogue, where he could preach the gospel to those who would be familiar with the messianic prophesies, but in Pisidian Antioch he met opposition from the Jews and turned to the Gentiles (Acts 13:44–46). Luke goes on to report the results: "And when the Gentiles heard this, they began rejoicing and glorifying the word of the Lord, and as many as were appointed to eternal life believed" (v. 48). Titus may have been one of those Gentiles, and when Paul again passed through Pisidian Antioch on the return trip, perhaps Paul decided Titus was ideal evidence for his sponsoring church in Syrian Antioch. This is all conjecture, of course, but when Paul and Barnabas gathered the Syrian Antioch church together to report "how [God] had opened a door of faith to the Gentiles" (Acts 14:27), perhaps Titus was there as proof.

EMISSARY TO CORINTH

Scripture does not indicate where Titus went after the Jerusalem Council. It is reasonable to assume that he accompanied Paul and Silas on the second missionary trip to the Gentiles, probably in early AD 50. We can be fairly certain, however, that he did not remain with Paul and Silas as far as Troas because it was there Luke joined Paul's entourage (Acts 16:8–10). Revisiting the churches he and Barnabas had founded, Paul would find Titus useful in relating the decision of the apostles and elders in Jerusalem (Acts 16:4), but he may have wanted Titus to leave the team when they reached his home city (perhaps Pisidian Antioch or Iconium). In fact, Titus's impending departure may have been the reason Paul recruited Timothy in Lystra (Acts 16:1–3).

The next reference to Titus places him in Ephesus with Paul during the apostle's third missionary trip. Beginning in AD 53, Paul began his third journey as he had the second, revisiting the churches of the Asia Minor interior. When he reached Titus's hometown, he may have invited Titus to rejoin him.

As we saw in our study of Prisca and Aquila, the city of Corinth, despite its somewhat sordid reputation and frontier atmosphere, became one of the two cities where Paul spent the longest time and which he continued to shepherd over the years. Another city close to Paul's heart was Ephesus, a major port city on the southwestern coast of modern Turkey. Paul saw an enormous opportunity in Ephesus. He had already installed Aquila and Prisca there as an advance team, but the work would require as many disciples as possible.

While in Ephesus, Paul received disturbing news from Corinth concerning divisions within the church.

📖 Read 1 Corinthians 1:11–24 and respond to the following questions.

What is the source of the problem in Corinth?

DIVISIONS VS 12ⁱⁿ WHOM THEY WERE FOLLOWING

What happens when a church is divided?

The congregation in Corinth had divided into groups claiming loyalty to a particular teacher—Peter (Cephas), Apollos, or Paul. The problems Paul addresses in 1 Corinthians—hair styles (11:6–15), tolerance (5:1–2), lawsuits (6:1–8), congregational meals (11:17–22), marriage (7:12–16), gender roles (14:34–36), food (8:1–13), and others—suggest church members more intent upon proving their spiritual superiority than sharing the gospel with the lost of Corinth. By dividing Christ, the Corinthians had become an ineffective conduit for the gospel.

Did You Know?

? EARLY CHRISTIAN GATHERINGS

Today, most Christians would have a distinct sense of familiarity at most worship services—a few hymns, a prayer or two, a sermon, and perhaps Communion—but how does our modern order of worship compare to first-century practices? First Corinthians is our only biblical glimpse into the practices of early Christians at their gatherings, but Paul is addressing problems. For other extrabiblical descriptions, you might explore two second-century documents—the letter of Pliny the Younger to Emperor Trajan (about AD 117) and Justin's *First Apology* (about AD 140). Both are available on the web at early-christianwritings.com and other sites.

As you look around the Christian world today, in what ways does the situation mirror that in first-century Corinth?

I AM A CATHOLIC, PROTESTANT, METHODISH ECT

When Paul had first visited Corinth during his second missionary journey, he had been accompanied by Silas and Timothy, among others. Now, Paul sent young Timothy across the Aegean to deliver his letter and work with the Corinthians. When Timothy was apparently unsuccessful in unifying the Corinthians and restoring their respect for Paul, he sent a second emissary—Titus (2 Corinthians 12:18).

What does Paul's dispatch of Titus suggest about the man?

TRUSTWORTHY, PROBLEM SOLVER,

Titus had apparently shown himself to be an attentive listener and a gentle teacher, yet one who was able to confront difficult people effectively. So Paul decided to proceed from Ephesus to Alexandria Troas, another strategically placed city, while Titus made a last-ditch effort in Corinth.

Paul was so anxious to hear the results of Titus's efforts in Corinth that he cut short his ministry in Troas and proceeded to Macedonia, where he encountered Titus on the road. It was a joyous reunion for Paul because Titus had good news.

📖 Read 2 Corinthians 7:6–7.

What had Titus accomplished in Corinth?

COMFORT AND PEACE REASSURANCE OF PAUL'S CARE FOR THEM, HIS SADNESS OVER THEIR DIVIDING AND HIS REJOICING TO HEAR OF REUNITING

He had succeeded in restoring the Corinthians' love and respect for Paul. Despite the problems within the Corinthian church, Titus must have found a place he felt he could contribute, so he asked Paul if he could return there (2 Corinthians 8:16–17).

FIFTH MISSIONARY JOURNEY

L uke's narrative of the early church in **Acts** ends abruptly with Paul's two-year house arrest in Rome (Acts 28:30–31), probably AD 60–62, but from information in his pastoral letters to Timothy and Titus, as well as some extrabiblical information, we know the apostle's story did not end there.

Well-attested tradition suggests Paul was beheaded by Nero in AD 66 or 67 as a scapegoat for the great fire of Rome in AD 64, so we have four or five

HOW MANY LETTERS?

While our Bible contains only two letters from Paul to the church in Corinth, many biblical scholars suggest 2 Corinthians is actually a combination of as many as four separate documents.

Titus

DAY THREE

unaccounted-for years. The clues to Paul's whereabouts during that time come from a variety of sources, and reconstructing his activities requires a treasure hunt (and a little speculation).

📖 Read Romans 15:24–28. When Paul wrote Romans from Ephesus in about AD 56, where did he hope to visit?

_____

_____

_____

Besides Rome, where the church had begun to take root despite a lack of apostolic leadership, Paul had ambitions to carry the gospel further west to Spain.

In about AD 98, a leader of the Roman church named Clement sent a letter to the church in Corinth, in which he wrote, "After preaching both in the east and west, [Paul] gained the illustrious reputation due to his faith, having taught righteousness to the whole world, and come to the extreme limit of the west, and suffered martyrdom under the prefects" (1 Clement 5).

If you look at a map of the Mediterranean world, where would the "extreme limit of the west" be to a Roman?

_____

_____

_____

West of the Italian peninsula lies Iberia, the location of Spain and Portugal. Furthermore, in the apocryphal *Acts of Peter*, there are two references to Paul's departure from Rome to Spain. Hence, there is ample reason to believe Paul ministered in Spain.

📖 Read Titus 1:4–5. Paul and Titus went together to the island of Crete.

📖 Read 2 Timothy 4:9–12. Titus had been with Paul sometime after Paul's first Roman imprisonment but now was in Dalmatia, a Roman province located along the northeastern Adriatic Sea (southern Albania and Serbia). If Titus came to Rome, Paul almost certainly would have welcomed his presence on the mission to Spain, where for the first time he would venture outside the range of the Jewish Diaspora. A Gentile partner would be an asset, even if he had no personal knowledge of Iberia. The trip to Crete may therefore have occurred immediately after the Spanish mission.

📖 Read 2 Timothy 4:20. This passage implies Paul had been in Corinth with Erastus.

📖 Read Titus 3:12. Neapolis was in the province of Epirus on the west coast of the Greek peninsula, south of Dalmatia.

Additional comments in 2 Timothy suggest Paul visited Corinth and Miletus (4:20), as well as Troas (4:13), between his first and second Roman imprisonments.

Did You Know?

PAUL'S TRAVELS

Today, many Westerners travel extensively, but it might surprise you to learn that many ancient Romans took long vacations. It was relatively common, for example, for wealthy Romans to visit many sites around the Mediterranean world. Even so, Paul's travels are remarkable for his time. In all he traveled at least 13,000 miles (about half by land and half by sea).

APPLY From these clues can you reconstruct Paul's travels after being released from Roman confinement in about AD 62?

_____

_____

_____

_____

Here's one of many possible scenarios:
- Paul and Titus (and probably others) sailed west from Rome and visit Spain.
- After a lengthy stay in Iberia, Paul and Titus sailed east to Crete.
- Paul left Titus in Crete and took the short voyage to Corinth.
- From Corinth, Paul traveled north along the eastern coast of the Greek peninsula to Neapolis, where Titus rejoined him.
- Titus traveled from Neapolis northward into Dalmatia while Paul returned to Philippi.
- From Philippi, Paul returned along the southern route through Macedonia and Achaia to Corinth.
- After a visit in Corinth, Paul crossed the Aegean to Ephesus.
- From Ephesus, he journeyed northward through Miletus to Troas. There he was recaptured by Roman authorities for transport to Rome, where he was eventually executed in about AD 67.

While details are a matter of speculation, Paul's undocumented fifth missionary journey may have been his longest—both in time and distance.

Word Study
PARTNER

Paul description of Titus as a *koinonos* (partner) comes from an important class of words with the root word *koinois* (common) from which we also get *koinoneo* (to share with others) and *koinonia* (fellowship). These words are used about the early Christians in Acts 2:42: "They devoted themselves to the apostles' teaching and fellowship [*koinonia*], to the breaking of bread and the prayers" and 2:44: "All who believed were together and had all things in common [*koinois*]."

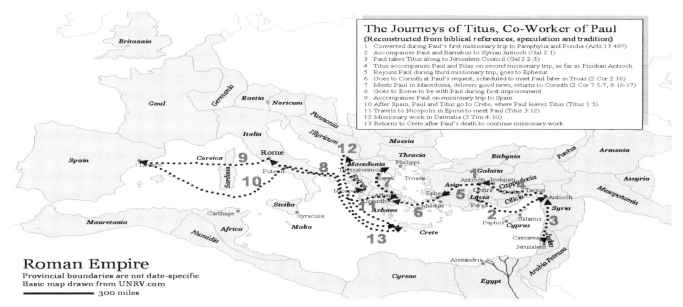

The Journeys of Titus, Co-Worker of Paul
(Reconstructed from biblical references, speculation and tradition)
1 Converted during Paul's first missionary trip to Pamphylia and Pisidia (Acts 13:48?)
2 Accompanies Paul and Barnabus to Syrian Antioch (Gal 2:1)
3 Paul takes Titus along to Jerusalem Council (Gal 2:2-3)
4 Titus accompanies Paul and Silas on second missionary trip, as far as Pisidian Antioch
5 Rejoins Paul during third missionary trip, goes to Ephesus
6 Goes to Corinth at Paul's request, scheduled to meet Paul later in Troas (2 Cor 2:18)
7 Meets Paul in Macedonia, delivers good news, returns to Corinth (2 Cor 7:5-7, 8:16-17)
8 Goes to Rome to be with Paul during first imprisonment
9 Accompanies Paul on missionary trip to Spain
10 After Spain, Paul and Titus go to Crete, where Paul leaves Titus (Titus 1:5)
11 Travels to Nicopolis in Epirus to meet Paul (Titus 3:12)
12 Missionary work in Dalmatia (2 Tim 4:10)
13 Returns to Crete after Paul's death to continue missionary work

Roman Empire
Provincial boundaries are not date-specific
Basic map drawn from UNRV.com
300 miles

These clues to Paul's whereabouts after his release from Roman captivity in about AD 62 allow us to get a very revealing glimpse into Titus's importance in Paul's later years. When the apostle urged Titus to return to Corinth six years earlier (2 Corinthians 8:6), he referred to him as his *"partner"* (v. 23). This is characteristic of Paul. Some see him as an autocratic leader, dispatching associates at his whim, but closer examination reveals that Paul never ordered his co-workers around—he urged them or encouraged them while leaving the final decision to them. This is clear in the case of Titus's return to Corinth when Paul testifies that his partner is doing so *"of his own accord"* (vv. 16, 17).

A DIFFICULT ASSIGNMENT

Titus had a passion for Corinth, but it is apparent he also had a passion for Paul's ministry to the Gentiles. We know he accompanied Paul to Crete (Titus 1:4–5) and remained there when Paul moved along. Paul apparently found the people of Crete rather distasteful.

📖 Read Titus 1:10–16.
If Paul made such a blanket statement about a group of people today, how do you think it would be received?

PREJUDIST.

The philosopher Paul quotes is Epimenides, himself a Cretan who lived in the sixth century BC, and there is an obvious logical inconsistency in the statement when uttered by a Cretan: "All Cretans [liars] are liars," says a Cretan (a liar). But neither Epimenides nor Paul apparently intended the paradox. Paul frequently used local culture in making his case for the gospel. In this case, once again, Paul's comments are directed primarily at the circumcision party, the Judaizers. Later in his letter to Titus, Paul softens the harshness directed at Cretans.

📖 Read Titus 3:1–3.
How does this statement affect Paul's use of the Epimenides quote?

Paul recognizes all people are sinners, and he considered himself the foremost (1 Timothy 1:15). He is simply pointing out the Cretans suffer from mankind's common maladies.

While Paul may not have been overly found of Cretans and had difficulties dealing with them while he was in Crete, he still had a passion for the Cretans' salvation. He left perhaps his most trusted partner behind to minister to them and gave him a threefold prescription for curing what ailed them. Read the passages listed below and write down Paul's three important instructions to Titus.

Titus 1:5–8. ORDER THINGS THAT ARE LACKING & APPOINT ELDERS

Titus 2:1–6. OLDER MEN, WOMEN, YOUNG WOMEN & MEN HOW TO BEHAVE

Titus 2:7. SHOWING YOURSELF AS A PATTERN OF GOOD WORKS & DOCTRINE

Paul's advice—identify qualified leaders, teach the truth, and practice what you preach—might not be a panacea for all ailing churches, but it's a good start.

When Paul asked Titus to join him in Nicopolis (Titus 3:12), he did not leave the Cretans without strong leadership. He intended to send one of two men, Artemas or Tychicus, to replace Titus. Artemas is not mentioned elsewhere in Scripture, but Tychicus is another close, long-standing associate of Paul's. He carried the letters of Colossians and Philemon to the church in Colossae (Colossians 4:7) and later was one of Paul's fellow travelers at the end of the apostle's third missionary journey (Acts 20:4–5). Still later, he bore Paul's letter to the Ephesian church (Ephesians 6:21).

Apparently, Paul was planning a missionary foray into Illyricum, and Tychicus was with him. That Paul chose to send Tychicus (or Artemas) to Crete and to wait for Titus before proceeding speaks volumes of Paul's confidence in Titus.

AM I A TRUSTED PARTNER?

Titus deserves more recognition from the church today, which suffers too much from a celebrity mentality. All leaders are susceptible to sin, and the best of them readily acknowledge this, but the degree to which the church suffers when one stumbles is evidence of our all-too-centralized view of the church. The church is intended to be an organism with only one head, Christ Jesus, and when we look too-devotedly to men (or women), the consequence is almost inevitable. The solution lies not in trying to be a Peter or a Paul but someone like a Titus—a trusted partner.

What does it take to become as trusted as Titus?

1. **It takes** _____. Titus's association with Paul lasted nearly twenty years (about AD 47–68). The biblical record shows that their relationship grew over the years—Titus going from an enthusiastic new convert to a trusted partner. The closeness they experienced doesn't usually happen overnight. To develop a meaningful relationship with others, we must be willing to invest our *time*.

2. **It takes** _____. During their twenty-year association, Titus and Paul were together for several extended periods: from the time of Titus's conversion on Paul's first missionary journey through the first part of the second (about AD 47–50), including the Jerusalem Council; in Ephesus and again in Macedonia during Paul's third mission (about AD 53–56); on Paul's final (post-Roman imprisonment) journey to Spain and Crete (about AD 63–65); and finally in Nicopolis shortly before Paul's rearrest and execution (about AD 67). We must spend a significant amount of face-to-face time, particularly working cooperatively in God's service, if we want a close relationship. *Proximity* is another key to developing trust.

3. **It takes** _____. Paul exhibited some immediate trust in Titus by bringing him to Jerusalem for the meeting with the apostles and elders in AD 49, but Titus's role appears to have been minor. During that and subsequent experiences, however, Titus obviously proved himself trustworthy. In about AD 55, Paul sent him to Corinth, the church for which the apostle had the deepest emotions, to reason with the Corinthians. Titus's success lifted Paul's downtrodden spirit and definitively verified his integrity and effectiveness in even the most difficult circumstances—so much so that Paul took him to Spain (probably) and to Crete (certainly), places that presented new challenges to Paul's evangelism. Developing trust isn't simply a matter of time and proximity; it is only confirmed through *results*.

The focus here has been Titus's role as Paul's trusted partner, but there is an even more important relationship for all of us—one embodied in a simple statement Paul made to the Corinthians: *"For we are God's fellow workers. You are God's field, God's building"* (1 Corinthians 3:9).

To be God's co-worker and partner carries the same requirements—time, proximity, and results.

If we want to be trusted partners with God, we need to access these aspects of our relationship. Ask yourself these questions:

APPLY   Do you give God your time?

_____

_____

_____

Do you create opportunities to get close to God?

_____

_____

_____

Are your spiritual results fruitful?

_____

_____

_____

If your response to any of those questions was no, what can you do to become a more trusted partner?

_____

_____

_____

_____

_____

_____

7

John Mark
Preparedness

Mark is certainly best known as the writer of the second Gospel in the New Testament, although chronologically the Gospel of Mark is almost universally considered the earliest written account of Jesus Christ (more on his Gospel on Day Four of this lesson). Some traditions make Mark the founder of the church in Alexandria and its first bishop, but the biblical references to him do not support this assertion. The development of individual bishops of cities did not emerge until at least the middle of the second century, long after Mark's death. The biblical references to Mark, however, leave significant gaps, so it is not impossible that he visited Alexandria and contributed to the development of the church there. On the other hand, neither Clement nor Origen (noted early Alexandrian church writers of the second and third centuries) make any mention of Mark.

Another tradition links Mark to the young man who fled naked from Gethsemane when Judas Iscariot led Roman soldiers to Jesus (Mark 14:51–52). More importantly, ancient testimony suggests Mark's Gospel came from the recollections of none other than the apostle Peter and that John Mark accompanied Peter on an unrecorded trip to Rome in about AD 42.

Briefly reconstructing Mark's life depends not only on that tradition but also on the date of Paul's letters to Colossae (Colossians and Philemon). While these have traditionally been

Put Yourself In Their Shoes
JOHN MARK

A Palestinian Jew who probably met Paul when Barnabas and the apostle brought relief to Jerusalem from the Antioch church in about AD 47.

"Epaphras, my fellow prisoner in Christ Jesus, sends greetings to you, and so do Mark, Aristarchus, Demas, and Luke, my fellow workers." (Philemon 23–24)

assigned to Paul's first Roman imprisonment (AD 60–62), some interpreters suggest they were more likely written during an unrecorded imprisonment in Ephesus following the riot of the silversmiths (about AD 56). Using that scenario, the known (and implied) highlights of Mark's life may be reconstructed as follows.

about 15-17	Born in Jerusalem to Mary, perhaps the sister of Barnabas
30	Present at the arrest of Jesus in Gethsemane; fled naked when the crow arrived.
42	May have accompanied Peter to Rome.
47	Went to Antioch with Paul and Barnabas.
47-48	Accompanied Paul and Barnabas to Cyprus on Paul's first missionary journey but returned to Jerusalem at Paphos or Perga.
49	Accompanied Barnabas to Cyprus after Paul refused to take him along on his second missionary journey.
	Traveled in Asia (modern Turkey).
about 56	With Paul in Ephesus and may have gone to Colossae at Paul's direction.
about 64	Paul asked Timothy to bring Mark to Rome.

Did You Know?

WHY TWO NAMES?

Among Hellenized Jews (those who lived in the Greco-Roman world) in particular, it was common for individuals to have both a Jewish and a Greek or Roman name. There are at least two examples other than John Marcus (the Greek version of Mark) in the New Testament—most notably, Saul Paulus and Jesus Justus (Colossians 4:11), an obscure co-worker of Paul's.

CHURCH KID

The first mention of John Mark by name occurs in Acts 12:12, where the house to which Peter went immediately after he was released from prison by an angel is identified as belonging to *"Mary, the mother of John whose other name was Mark."*

📖 Read Acts 12:6–12.

Why might Peter go to Mary's house upon his release?

_____

_____

_____

_____

Peter's instinct to go there implies Mary's house was a routine gathering place for the church in Jerusalem, and it is also believed to have been the site of the upper room where Jesus and His disciples celebrated the Passover meal and where the disciples gathered on the occasion of the coming of the Holy Spirit.

📖 Read Mark 14:12–15.

Assuming the house where the Jesus and the disciples ate the Passover meal (now referred to as the Last Supper) belonged to Mary, what can we infer about Mary from this passage?

_____

_____

_____

Because the house is referred to as Mary's (Acts 12:12) and not her husband's, Mary was probably a widow, and having a house with an upper room large enough to accommodate a substantial number of guests suggests she was relatively wealthy. Furthermore, she certainly knew Jesus and the disciples well.

📖 Read Acts 1:12–14; 2:1–6.

Describe what you think it would have been like to be in that house that day.

_____

_____

_____

_____

Being touched by miraculous fire must have been initially terrifying. After all, throughout Scripture, people respond to supernatural events such as a visitation by an angel with fear. Confusion followed the fear as the disciples began to speak in unfamiliar languages. Finally, when they began to realize they had been given something very special, they must have been filled with awe, remembering Jesus' promise to send a counselor.

We don't really know if the upper room was in Mary's house, but the tradition is strong. If all these events (the Last Supper, the coming of the Holy Spirit on Pentecost, and Peter's report of his miraculous escape) all occurred at Mary's house, Mark would have witnessed (or at least been aware of) profoundly significant events.

John Mark was probably a very young man at the time of these events (about thirteen or fourteen) making him perhaps the first "church kid"—someone who grew up surrounded by the stories of Jesus.

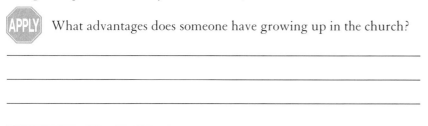 What advantages does someone have growing up in the church?

_____

_____

_____

_____

Personally, I didn't grow up in a home with a strong Christian tradition. I went to church on a fairly regular basis until I was twelve or so, learning the familiar Bible stories in Sunday school, but that was pretty much the end of my religious experience until twenty-five years later. I sometimes envy (in a positive way) my friends who grew up in a committed Christian home where they began hearing and memorizing Scripture about the same time they learned to talk. I've had a lot of catching up to do!

MARY'S HOUSE

The Syrian Bishopric headquarters in Jerusalem occupies a traditional site of Mary's house in Jerusalem.

Did You Know?

PENTECOST

Today, _Pentecost_ (fiftieth day) is a notable day on the Christian calendar, celebrated as the day the Holy Spirit came to the disciples in the upper room, seven weeks after Easter. But Pentecost was also one of the most important Jewish holidays—the Festival of Weeks (or Reaping or First Fruits)—mandated in the Mosaic law. Tied to Passover (as Pentecost is tied to Easter), the Festival of Weeks is described in Leviticus 23:5–21.

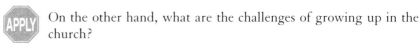

APPLY On the other hand, what are the challenges of growing up in the church?

_____

_____

_____

As flawed humans, we often long to see if the grass is really greener on the other side of the hill, and the statistics on the faithfulness of individuals who grow up in a committed Christian home are not as reassuring as I would like as a parent. One of the things that attracted the earliest followers of Jesus was the novelty of His message—how it often flew in the face of the prevailing religious attitudes of His day. With their familiarity with the gospel, church kids may miss out on the incredible sense of newness a later initial encounter with Jesus brings.

📖 Read 1 Corinthians 7:13–14.

What does Paul say about the children of even just one believing parent?

_____

_____

It is wonderfully comforting as parents to get this assurance our children are holy (set apart) by our belief, but this is not necessarily lifelong protection. Most children inevitably question their parents' values. On the whole, however, I think children from Christian homes have a decided spiritual advantage in our difficult society. Even if the siren call of the world distracts them at some point, they have a foundation of truth.

FAILURE

The first few years of Paul's life as a Christian following his encounter with the risen Jesus on the Damascus Road (Acts 9:1–9) are difficult to reconstruct with any certainty. He apparently spent about three years in Damascus and Arabia before traveling to Jerusalem for a two-week visit with Peter (Galatians 1:18). Because Paul (Saul) had been a determined persecutor of the church, he encountered fear and skepticism from many in the Judean church, but Barnabas's testimony reassured some, and Paul began preaching in Jerusalem. Very quickly, Jewish leaders in the city viewed him as the ultimate traitor and sought to kill him, so the church dispatched him back to his hometown of Tarsus, where he had no known contact with the Jerusalem church for the next ten years or so.

How do you think Paul dealt with this long separation from the church and the disciples?

_____

_____

_____

_____

John Mark

DAY TWO

After his conversion, Paul went east to Arabia for three years before visiting Jerusalem. Because of threats to his life, he returned to Tarsus, where he remained until Barnabas came years later and took him to Antioch.

Neither Luke nor Paul (in his autobiographical narrative in Galatians 1:14–2:1) reveals anything about the apostle's activities during that period. When Paul wrote to the church in Corinth in AD 56, he told of a profound spiritual experience he had fourteen years earlier—being *"caught up to the third heaven"* (see 2 Corinthians 12:1–6)—placing that event about in the middle of his time in Tarsus. Clearly, the Holy Spirit was preparing Paul for the great work on which he would later embark. His activities, however, are a mystery. By the turn of the century, we know there was a viable Christian community in Tarsus, but we don't know of its beginnings.

In AD 46, reports of Christian activity in Antioch reached the Jerusalem church, and the leaders sent Barnabas to investigate. When Barnabas saw the evidence of a thriving, largely Gentile church, he must have remembered Saul, and he went on to Tarsus to bring him to Antioch (Acts 11:22–25). For the next year, Barnabas and Saul taught in the Antioch church until a man named Agabus prophesied a great famine. Apparently Antioch was spared the worst of the disaster and decided to send money to the brothers and sisters in Judea. The elders of the church in Antioch chose Barnabas and Saul to deliver this relief (Acts 11:26–30).

What does the elders' decision tell us about Paul?

_____

_____

_____

During his year in Antioch, Paul had obviously earned the trust of the church. When he and Barnabas returned from Jerusalem, they brought along John Mark (Acts 12:25). Shortly thereafter, the Holy Spirit spoke to some of the Antioch church leaders during a time of worship, telling them it was time for Paul and Barnabas to begin the work for which they had been prepared (Acts 13:1–3)—the mission to spread the gospel among the Gentiles. They went first to the island of Cyprus, bringing John Mark along.

John Mark's specific role on the missionary trip is unclear. By this time (AD 47 or 48), he was probably in his earlier thirties—still a young man by contemporary Jewish standards, hardly a "baby Christian." Luke describes him as a *hupēretēs* to Paul and Barnabas, a word literally meaning "an under-oarsman," which seems to connote an assistant. But the word is translated elsewhere as *"officer"*, *"servant"*, *"attendant"*, and *"minister."*

📖 Read Acts 13:5. Based on this verse, what do you think John Mark's role was?

_____

_____

_____

The immediate context of the passage is preaching in the Salamis synagogues, so it does not appear Mark was some sort of valet or personal assistant. I think Saul and Barnabas brought him along as an assistant preacher. John Mark was at the beginning of a promising career as a Christian evangelist accompanying the apostle Paul.

Did You Know?

CYPRUS

The island of Cyprus was the first stop on Paul's first missionary journey, accompanied by Barnabas and John Mark. The distance between Salamis and Paphos is about seventy-five miles. When the team sailed to Perga, northwest of Cyprus on the coast of Pamphylia (now part of Turkey), Mark left.

📖 Read Acts 13:13. In the space of eight verses, representing perhaps a month or two, Mark's missionary career seems to come to an end. Why might John Mark have left Paul and Barnabas?

_____

_____

_____

Yet another tantalizing detail about which we can only speculate. Perhaps John Mark never intended to be gone from Jerusalem for long, so after a couple of months on Cyprus he decided it was time to go home. Parenthetically, this is another of those embarrassing details that support the validity of the New Testament documents—a Gospel writer who abandoned a missionary trip.

I think there may have been several factors contributing to John Mark's decision:
• Fear. From early on, as evidenced by Elymas the magician (Acts 13:8), Paul and Barnabas encountered opposition.
• Weak faith. Having grown up as a "church kid," perhaps Mark had just not developed his own independent faith sufficiently to stand up to a challenge.
• Cognitive dissonance. John Mark accompanied Paul and Barnabas to Antioch and its Gentile church, but it doesn't appear he was there long. Now, with Sergius Paulus (Acts 13:7), he witnessed Paul preaching to a Gentile! For years, John Mark had been surrounded by the Jerusalem church made up predominantly or exclusively of Jews. Like some Christians in Judea, he may have assumed Jesus' message was meant only for his people.

Whatever the reason, it wasn't good enough for Paul.

📖 Read Acts 15:35–41.

What does Paul's reaction tell you about John Mark's departure?

_____

_____

_____

The _"sharp disagreement"_ may say more about Paul than John Mark, although it's understandable, given Paul's complete commitment to the gospel, that he would not want to risk depending on someone who had already proven undependable, particularly since Mark hadn't even experienced the harrowing events Paul and Barnabas subsequently went through, particularly in Lystra (see Acts 14:8–19).

Why do you think Barnabas was more charitable toward John Mark?

_____

_____

The answer may lie in two passages:
• _"Thus Joseph, who was also called by the apostles Barnabas (which means son of encouragement)..."_ (Acts 4:36). Barnabas was so well-known for his support and encouragement of others, the apostles renamed him. As an encourager, Barnabas would be far more likely to give a person a second chance.

Did You Know?

A NEW NAME

Barnabas was not the only Christian to get a new name. Most famously, Jesus gave Simon the name Peter, (or Cephas), meaning "rock" (John 1:42), and he called James and John _Boanerges_—"Sons of Thunder" (Mark 3:17). In the early church, it became common for Christians to take on new names, particularly slaves, whose masters often gave them names of ridicule.

- "Aristarchus my fellow prisoner greets you, and Mark the cousin of Barnabas (concerning whom you have received instructions—if he comes to you, welcome him)" (Colossians 4:10). Being related to John Mark, Barnabas would also want to give the young man another chance. (While the translation is "cousin," most commentators suggest John Mark was the son of Barnabas's sister Mary, and thus his nephew.)

Mark's missionary career continued, just not immediately with Paul. Whatever made John Mark leave Paul and Barnabas in Perga was apparently now in the past. Scripture is silent about the trip Barnabas and John Mark took to Cyprus or where they went from there, but there are hints strongly suggesting John Mark later restored himself with Paul.

RESTORATION

In AD 64 or so, Paul was brought to Rome a second time. During his previous two-year confinement (60–62), he had been treated well, given private accommodations and open visitation by friends. He had hoped to testify before the emperor, but his case was probably viewed at the time as so trivial not to merit Nero's attention. Now, everything had changed. Dogged by rumors he had ordered the devastating fire in Rome in AD 63, Nero sought scapegoats, and he chose the nefarious new superstition known as Christianity. Someone may have reminded him that one of its primary leaders had once been in his custody, so Nero ordered Paul brought back to Rome. This time, there was little hope of release, as reflected in Paul's final letter, 2 Timothy. Near the end of that letter, Paul mentions John Mark.

📖 Read 2 Timothy 4:9–11.

What is Paul's attitude toward John Mark now?

_____

_____

_____

_____

When we hear Paul say that Mark is *"useful to me for ministry [or service],"* we might get the impression of a helper serving Paul's needs, but Paul didn't care about his comfort: *"I know how to be brought low, and I know how to abound. In any and every circumstance, I have learned the secret of facing plenty and hunger, abundance and need. I can do all things through him who strengthens me"* (Philippians 4:12–13).

Also notice what else Paul says: *"Get Mark"* (2 Timothy 4:11). Paul is writing to Timothy in Ephesus, and it is clear Mark isn't there, although Paul (and Timothy) seems to know where he is. Paul wants Timothy to do his best *"to come to me soon,"* (v. 9), yet he wants Timothy to go to wherever Mark is and bring him along.

Despite being in prison and facing the likelihood of execution, Paul is still thinking first about how he can advance the preaching of the gospel. His

Robert Hubert, *The Burning of Rome*, (1733–1808)

In AD 63, a massive fire devastated much of Rome. The historian Tacitus reported, "Of Rome's fourteen districts only four remained intact. Three were leveled to the ground. The other seven were reduced to a few scorched and mangled ruins." Tacitus's history is also the source of the myth that Nero fiddled while Rome burned. In fact, Nero led initial relief efforts by opening up public grounds, including his gardens, to the homeless. But Tacitus also wrote, "A rumor had spread that, while the city was burning, Nero had gone on his private stage and, comparing modern calamities with ancient, had sung of the destruction of Troy."

choice for the person to best help him do so is the man who had abandoned him in Perga sixteen years earlier! What had John Mark done in those years to earn such respect from Paul?

📖 Read Colossians 4:7–11; Philemon 23–24.
What do you learn about John Mark from these passages?

_____

_____

_____

Colossians and Philemon are companion letters, delivered to Colossae (where Philemon lived) by Tychicus. We'll return to these letters again in the last chapter of this study, but for now it's useful to know Paul wrote them from jail—either during an unrecorded imprisonment in Ephesus (about AD 56) or during his first Roman imprisonment (AD 60–62). In both letters, he adds Mark's greeting to the recipients, telling us:
• John Mark is with him in Ephesus or Rome.
• John Mark is known to the Christians in Colossae.
• Paul expects John Mark to visit Colossae soon, and he has given the Colossians instructions about him.
• Mark's work has been enough to earn Paul's commendation as a co-worker.

As a man of action himself, Paul valued action in others. When Mark failed at the beginning of the first missionary journey, Paul was sufficiently disappointed to split with Barnabas, the man who had supported him in Jerusalem, sought him out in Tarsus, taught alongside him in Antioch, and accompanied him with relief for Jerusalem.

The conclusion is inescapable—during the eight years or so between Mark's departure from Perga and Paul's presumed confinement in Ephesus, Mark had proven to be a courageous and effective spokesman for the gospel. Another eight years later, as Paul awaits execution in Rome, Mark is still in his mind, suggesting Mark had continued tireless work.

If we disappoint others by our lack of commitment, courage, energy, or whatever, we can find the relationship between Paul and John Mark an antidote for our failure and an enormous source of encouragement.

THE FIRST GOSPEL

Commentators and scholars are virtually unanimous in the opinion Mark's Gospel is the earliest written account of Jesus' life and ministry. The Gospels of Matthew, Mark, and Luke are known as the synoptic gospels because of the great degree of overlap between them. Literary evidence strongly suggests both Matthew and Luke used Mark's Gospel as a source for their own. According to the second-century Christian writer Papias (about AD 130, as quoted by Eusebius about AD 325), "Mark neither heard the Lord nor followed him"; that is, he was not an eyewitness to the events about which he wrote (probably because of his youth at the time). If so, where did Mark get his information about Jesus?

PAUL ON WORK

Paul frequently commended people for the works of service they performed on behalf of the cause of Christ. For example, in Romans 16, he names a lot of Roman Christians, citing two women, Mary and Persis, for their hard work. Paul insisted salvation was God's gift: _"For by grace you have been saved through faith. And this is not your own doing; it is the gift of God, not a result of works, so that no one may boast"_ (Ephesians 2:8–9). But his attitude toward work demonstrates that he certainly agreed with James: _"Faith by itself, if it does not have works, is dead"_ (James 2:17).

John Mark

DAY FOUR

We've already seen that Mark's mother, Mary, was a significant figure in the early Jerusalem church, but Papias claims Mark was "the interpreter of Peter, and wrote down accurately, though not in order, the teaching of Peter." Before Mark became associated with Paul, therefore, it seems he was Peter's student. No one else in the New Testament had close relationships with both figures in nascent Christianity—the apostle to the Jews *and* the apostle to the Gentiles!

Considerable tradition (although no certain proof) indicates that Peter traveled to Rome in about AD 42, and some suggest Mark traveled with him.

I suppose I'm dating myself with this, but Mark's Gospel might be called the Joe Friday (of *Dragnet* fame) Gospel of the synoptics—"Just the facts, ma'am." Although there are examples where Mark's version is more detailed than that of Matthew and Luke, Mark is generally more parsimonious with his words. There are ample print and Internet resources to explore comparisons between the synoptics, but one example may suffice.

📖 Read Mark 1:12–13; Matthew 4:1–11; Luke 4:1–13.
How might you account for the differences in these passages?

_____

_____

_____

Those who seek to disparage Christianity love to nitpick such differences. On the other hand, too many Christians deny the differences or construct elaborate explanations. The primary problem is really an anachronistic reading of the New Testament—one that expects first-century writers to adhere to the literary conventions of today.

Chronology is one good example of this. If you read the accounts of Jesus' temptation carefully, you may note a difference between Matthew and Luke. In both, there are three temptations, but these two Gospel writers cite a different order of the temptations.

 "Ah ha!" the skeptic says. "There it is! Your gospels aren't reliable because they don't agree." How would you respond?

_____

_____

_____

I have several church-history volumes, including W. H. C. Frend's classic *The Rise of Christianity* and Bill R. Austin's wonderful (but out-of-print) *Topical History of Christianity*. Because Frend arranges events chronologically and Austin topically, the placement of events differs in the two books. Does that make these histories unreliable?

The Gospel writers had different purposes and different audiences; they emphasize different things and sometimes rearrange events to address a particular topic. Furthermore, authors differ in the amount of detail provided. Frend devotes six pages to Marcion (a second-century heretic), while Austin has less than one full page. Clearly, Austin provides considerably less detail, but that does not make Frend's information inaccurate.

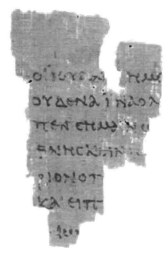

This papyrus fragment, known as *p52*, is currently the earliest New Testament document. Dated to AD 125, it is a portion of John 18. Before the discovery of this document, some cynics claimed the Gospel of John was written as late as the second half of the second century.

Skeptics love to make lists of supposed contradictions in the Bible. What does the word *contradiction* mean to you?

_____

_____

_____

Two statements contradict if one denies elements of the other or if the elements of each are incompatible. In no case I'm aware of does one Gospel writer directly contradict another in any way that would affect core Christian doctrine.

Another approach employed by those who seek to discredit Christianity is to move the writing of New Testament documents to as late a date as possible. There is strong evidence Paul was executed by Emperor Nero sometime between AD 65–67. Skeptics claim the date of Luke's Acts is as late as AD 130.

📖 Read Acts 28:30–31.

What is missing in Luke's account of Paul's ministry?

_____

_____

_____

There are probably lots of missing details. For example, in 2 Corinthians 11:23 (written in about AD 56), Paul writes he has experienced *"far more imprisonments"* than other apostles, yet in Acts only one imprisonment before AD 56 is reported (in Philippi, about AD 51). The absence of a specific detail does not invalidate the accuracy of the information included!

If Acts was written any time after AD 67, the most notable missing detail is Paul's death. Acts ends rather abruptly with Paul in jail (about AD 62). The suggestion by some that Luke omits Paul's execution because it's embarrassing is pure silliness. The execution of Stephen (Acts 6:8–7:60)—with Paul in attendance—and James (Acts 12:1–2) are included. Why are these less "embarrassing" than Paul's?

The almost inescapable conclusion is Paul's execution is not included in Acts because it had not yet happened when Luke finished his treatise on the early church. That places the date of Acts no later than AD 62 or 63. Since Luke's Gospel preceded Acts and Mark's Gospel preceded Luke's, the latest date of Mark is in the AD 50s.

The skeptics' purpose for pushing back the dates of New Testament writings is another example of anachronistic criticism, because it assumes the more years between an event and its recording, the less accurate the account is. But this ignores the role of oral tradition in ancient times. Today, particularly in the West, memorization and oral storytelling have largely disappeared, but in Mark's day, Jewish boys were expected to memorize the entire Torah (Genesis, Exodus, Leviticus, Numbers, and Deuteronomy).

HOW PREPARED AM I?

The events in John Mark's life provide many lessons on preparedness. He apparently was *not* prepared for mission work when he left Antioch with Paul and Barnabas in AD 47, but he clearly corrected his deficiency in the ensuing years.

On Day One of this lesson, we looked at the differences between growing up in a committed Christian environment (a "church kid") versus coming to faith later in life, as I did.

APPLY Which were you and what challenges did you face?

_____

_____

_____

_____

If you are a committed Christian now with a family, how can you give your children the best chance to remain faithful?

_____

_____

_____

_____

There's no one answer to a question like that, because it probably depends on your individual situation. My own church family focuses a lot on biblical knowledge, so for us, an answer might be to provide children with other types of spiritual experiences, such as missions where they can experience Christ on other ways.

On Day Two, we looked at John Mark's failure to see something through. He left Paul and Barnabas early in their mission to bring the gospel to the Gentile world.

APPLY In what ways have you let others down (we all do) in your Christian walk?

_____

_____

_____

_____

What did you do in response to your failure?

_____

_____

_____

_____

How have others let you down, and what did you do in response?

_____

_____

_____

Without being critical of Paul, particularly since John Mark eventually fulfilled Paul's hopes, I sometimes wonder what would have happened to John Mark had Barnabas not been around. Clearly, Barnabas got his name (son of encouragement) the hard way—he earned it. Try to take every opportunity to be a Barnabas to the people in your life.

On Day Three, we saw how John Mark ended up earning Paul's admiration and confidence.

APPLY What are the shortcomings in your life right now, and how can you overcome these?

_____

_____

_____

John Mark overcame his shortcomings by picking himself up and trying again. By the time Paul wrote about him in Colossians, it's clear he had become known to Christians in the important city of Colossae. It's not always a case, however, of redoing the same thing. We don't all have the same gifts. Perhaps if you have fallen short in one endeavor, you can excel at another.

On Day Four, we took a very brief look at the reliability of the Gospels and the attacks of those determined to denigrate Christianity. Peter wrote that we must always be _"prepared to make a defense_ [Greek _apologia_, from which we derive "apologetics"] _to anyone who asks you for a reason for the hope that is in you"_ (1 Peter 3:15).

APPLY What kind of defense are you prepared to give when asked?

_____

_____

_____

We're not all required to give detailed interpretations of biblical passages or to explain the meaning of the original Greek, but Peter's instruction is clear that we must all be prepared.

How could you be better prepared to make a defense?

_____

_____

_____

_____

_____

8

Philemon
Slave and Master

After recently reading Ken Follett's *World Without End*, a story of conflict between secular and religious forces in fourteenth-century England and sequel to his wonderful *The Pillars of the Earth*, I may never be able to respond to the name Philemon in the same way again. Follett's Philemon, you see, is one of the most despicable characters in the novel. Thankfully, Paul's Philemon is a far nobler individual, although the letter written to him was, for a period in American history, used to support our greatest national shame. More on that later.

Philemon lived in Colossae about one hundred miles east of Ephesus, in the fertile Lycus Valley. He is best known as the recipient of the most personal letter by Paul in the New Testament, from which we get all our information about him because he is not mentioned elsewhere. Philemon was apparently wealthy and, from Paul's comments, very loving, charitable, and faithful.

Put Yourself In Their Shoes
PHILEMON

Philemon (*fil-AH-mone*) was a citizen of Colossae whose name means "friendly."

He probably met Paul in Ephesus sometime during Paul's long residence, about AD 53–56.

"Paul, a prisoner for Christ Jesus, and Timothy our brother, To Philemon our beloved fellow worker." (Philemon 1)

Philemon

DAY ONE

A JERUSALEM GATE?

A common interpretation of Matthew 19:24, Mark 10:25, and Luke 18:25 suggests that the "eye of a needle" refers to a narrow gate into Jerusalem through which a camel could pass only with great difficulty or by unloading its cargo. Such an interpretation softens the meaning of the passage, but there is no evidence of such a gate. Jesus intended to convey the immense obstacle wealth is for salvation as He literally put it. The harsher understanding need not, however, be discouraging because Jesus' main point is that the wealthy need to rely on God, not on their wealth, in order to inherit eternal life.

THE WISE TEACHER

In many education circles, it is axiomatic that good teachers ask open-ended questions to stimulate discussion. I try to do that myself in my teaching, but I am often struck by how many closed-ended questions Jesus asked. Matthew 6:27 (also Luke 12:25) is one example of such a question: "_And which of you by being anxious can add a single hour to his span of life?_" That certainly does not mean Jesus was not a good teacher! Jesus taught the truth, so the opinions of others expressed in a discussion were of no consequence. He often led people to that truth through questions with only one answer. He insisted God is the only true teacher (Matthew 23:8).

THE EYE OF A NEEDLE

In this lesson, I assume Colossians and Ephesians were written from Ephesus.

There are a number of things people generally believe the Bible says that it doesn't (and many more things people wish it didn't). Foremost among misquoted Scripture is the claim that "money is the root of all evil." In a recent survey, 60 percent of respondents thought that was a direct quote from Jesus. While Jesus had a lot to say about money, he didn't say anything like that. The source of the saying is actually Paul, who wrote, "_The love of money is the root of all kinds of evils_" (1 Timothy 6:10).

For those of us in America (and more generally in the West), who control a disproportionate share of the world's wealth (in 2000, North American households—with 6 percent of the world's population—controlled a whopping 34 percent of the world's wealth), few subjects are more relevant than money.

During Jesus' ministry, a rich young man asked what he had to do to inherit eternal life. Jesus' response—to sell everything he had and give the proceeds to the poor—disheartened the young man, who went away sorrowful (Matthew 19:16–22, repeated almost verbatim in Mark 10:17–22 and Luke 18:18–23). Jesus used this incident to deliver his most important teaching about money.

📖 Read Matthew 19:23–30.

What does Jesus teach in this passage?

_____

_____

_____

_____

We can glean the following from this passage:
- Wealth places a spiritual burden on individuals.
- Salvation and eternal life are impossible for the wealthy without a relationship with God.
- There are eternal rewards for those who sacrifice wealth to further the kingdom of God.
- Those who reach the highest levels of status (by worldly standards) in this life will find themselves in the lowest levels in the afterlife.

📖 Read Matthew 6:24–34.

What financial principles do we learn from this passage?

_____

_____

_____

Christians are not to serve or worry about money. If we serve God, Jesus teaches us, God will supply our basic needs. Some in the early church apparently took teachings like this far too literally. In our study of Demas, we looked at Paul's reaction to those who stopped working and lived off church charity.

📖 Read 2 Thessalonians 3:10–12 again as a reminder.

Does Paul's advice in this passage contradict Jesus' teaching in Matthew 6:24–34? Why or why not?

_____

_____

_____

_____

Paul is not telling the Thessalonians to focus their attention on money, but he is critical of those who, despite having the means to support themselves, rely on the charity of others. Ostentatious wealth and self-inflicted poverty are two sides of the same sinful coin—displays of pride.

Philemon was apparently quite wealthy. He owned slaves. His house was large enough to accommodate Christian gatherings. Paul had never visited Colossae when he wrote to Philemon, so the two met elsewhere. The most likely location would be Ephesus, about one hundred miles west of Colossae along fine Roman roads. Ephesus was the primary trading port in Asia Minor, so Philemon may well have visited there often on business. On one of these trips, then, he may have met Paul, become a Christian, and worked alongside the apostle, but clearly Philemon did not sell everything he had and distribute it to the poor. Did he then face the challenge as difficult as a camel going through the eye of a needle to inherit eternal life?

📖 Read Philemon 4–7.

Did Philemon serve God or money?

_____

_____

_____

_____

Philemon's reputation as a man of love and charity who actively shared his faith with others had been reported to Paul, and Paul's love for Philemon was based not on what he had done for Paul but what he had done for others. _"The hearts of the saints have been refreshed through [Philemon]"_ (v. 7). By serving God first, Philemon is an example of someone who used his wealth for the cause of Christ.

EMPOWERING OTHERS

Philemon

DAY TWO

Again, Paul had not visited Colossae when he wrote Colossians and Philemon. How then had the gospel taken root in the Lycus Valley?

📖 Read Colossians 1:3–8.

What role did Epaphras play in Colossae?

_____

_____

_____

A MISSIONARY TRAINING SCHOOL

"But when some became stubborn and continued in unbelief, speaking evil of the Way before the congregation, (Paul) withdrew from them and took the disciples with him, reasoning daily in the hall of Tyrannus. This continued for two years, so that all the residents of Asia heard the word of the Lord, both Jews and Greeks." (Acts 19:9–10)

Obviously, not every resident of Asia traveled to Ephesus to hear Paul. One purpose of Paul's daily teaching in the hall of Tyrannus must have been to equip missionaries like Epaphras he could send out into the surrounding areas.

Paul traveled thousands of miles during his three-decade ministry, spreading the gospel across the Mediterranean world. Even so, he knew he could not do it alone—he needed co-workers. During his lengthy stay in Ephesus (about AD 53–56), therefore, he probably began training fellow missionaries, and Epaphras may well have been one of these, dispatched to the cities of the Lycus Valley (Colossae, Laodicea, and Hierapolis) to preach and teach.

Paul was not haphazard in his approach to evangelizing the Gentile world. There is ample evidence he planned out his travels. He writes of his intentions to visit Colossae (Philemon 22), Rome (Romans 1:15), and Spain (Romans 15:24). Over the years, he developed an evangelistic strategy he employed with increasing sophistication.

Before he visited a city, as noted above, he sometimes wrote an advance letter.

📖 Read Acts 18:18–19.

What strategy did Paul employ in Ephesus?

_____

_____

_____

On his first stop in Ephesus during his second missionary journey, Paul stayed only three weeks or so, but he brought his trusted co-workers, Prisca and Aquila, leaving them as a base team when he proceeded to Judea. He apparently did something similar later, sending Prisca and Aquila back to their original home in Rome before his planned visit.

📖 Read the following verses from Acts: 13:5, 14; 14:1; 17:1–2, 16–17; 18:1, 4, 19; 19:1, 8.

What did Paul do upon arriving in a city? Why?

_____

_____

_____

_____

Paul almost invariably went to the local Jewish synagogue to teach. There were probably at least three reasons for this strategy: Paul felt his first obligation was to his fellow Jews; Jews would have the scriptural knowledge of the things about which Paul taught from the law and the prophets; consequently, Jews would be the "easiest" converts from which to form a basis of a new church. Of course, Paul did not always get a positive response from his kinsmen, but there were usually at least a few Jews who accepted his message.

📖 Now read 1 Corinthians 9:19–23; Acts 17:22–23, 27–29; 1 Corinthians 15:33; and Titus 1:12.

Do you see a strategy in these passages?

_____

_____

_____

_____

Paul understood that reaching people often meant couching his message in familiar terms, so he sometimes used sources outside the Jewish Scriptures, such as an Athenian altar (Acts 17:22–23); the Cilician poet Aratus (Acts 17:27–29); the philosopher Menander (1 Corinthians 15:33), and the Cretan philosopher-prophet, Epimenides (Titus 1:12).

📖 Read Romans 16:1–2, 23; Acts 16:14; 17:34.

What did Paul do before leaving a city?

_____

_____

_____

_____

Paul certainly did not focus on wealthy, prominent people, but well-to-do believers like Phoebe, Gaius, Erastus, Lydia, Dionysius, and Philemon could host and support a new Christian community, providing an element of stability in a pagan world.

RESPONSIBILITY

I f Paul employed a strategy to establish churches in new communities, he was no less diligent in his ongoing responsibility, and he seems to have used three primary follow-up approaches.

📖 Read Acts 15:41; 20:1–2.

What did Paul do to help ensure the churches he founded would survive and thrive?

_____

_____

_____

Paul routinely revisited "his" churches. He went to Derby, Lystra, Iconium, and Pisidian Antioch twice on his first missionary trip, once on his second, and probably again on his third. He spent time in Philippi and Thessalonica on his second mission, twice each again on his third, and probably again between his first and second Roman imprisonments (about AD 62–64). Likewise, he first went to Corinth on his second mission, revisiting twice on

"To the Jews I became as a Jew, in order to win Jews. To those under the law I became as one under the law (though not being myself under the law) that I might win those under the law."

I Corinthians 9:20

Philemon

DAY THREE

his third, and again later. After his short visit to Ephesus at the end of his second mission (when he brought Aquila and Prisca), he came back for an extended period during the third missionary journey. At the very end of the third trip, he also summoned the Ephesian leadership to Miletus (a city about thirty miles south), where he addressed them. These repeat visits document Paul's commitment to the churches.

Paul's second follow-up strategy makes up a substantial portion of the New Testament—his letters to the churches and their individual leaders. With the exception of Romans (a pre-visit letter) and Philemon (a private letter), every epistle by Paul—whether addressed to a specific church (for example, Philippians), a group of churches (for example, Galatians), or a church leader (for example, 1 Timothy)—contains encouragement, advice, clarifications, and sometimes rebukes to the churches he directly or indirectly (for example, Colossae) founded.

Paul employed at least one more clear strategy in carrying out his responsibilities to the churches.

📖 Read Acts 17:14; 1 Corinthians 4:17; Acts 19:22; Philippians 2:19. What approach is Paul using?

_____

_____

_____

_____

Paul employed his associates—in this case, Timothy—to visit churches when he could not. Sometimes, such as the case of Corinth, the associate's visit was to address one or more problematic issues. Read the verses and fill in the table below for other examples of Paul's deployment of associates.

Passage	Associate	Destination
Acts 19:22		Macedonia
Acts 17:14		
Philippians 2:25	Epaphroditus	
Ephesians 6:21-22		
Titus 1:5		

APPLY If we can discern a clear set of strategies in Paul's evangelistic efforts, what do you learn from that?

_____

_____

_____

_____

_____

"That is why I sent you Timothy, my beloved and faithful child in the Lord, to remind you of my ways in Christ, as I teach them everywhere in every church."

I Corinthians 4:17

A Societal Disgrace

There is a practice employed in most Christian circles using individual Bible verses to justify sometimes unbiblical concepts. Known as proof texting, it can be used to justify just about anything.

The evolution of the New Testament canon makes a very interesting study, one that for me only served to reinforce my confidence in the reliability of the Bible. The term "canon" (Latin for measuring stick or standard) refers to the writings considered authoritative by the early church, mostly established in the first one hundred years after the resurrection and fully by the fourth century. These writings (Gospels, letters, and one revelation) became the New Testament, which serves as the standard by which all other writing and teaching are measured.

I believe the New Testament contains everything we need to have faith in God and Christ Jesus and to know what He asks of us. That is not to say there aren't very worthwhile writings—both ancient and modern—outside the Bible. Even before the church came to broad agreement on the contents of the canon, church leaders cited the value of other works. The *Letter of Barnabas*, the *Didache* (*Teaching of the Twelve*), and the *Apocalypse of Peter* are all examples of writings praised by one or more leaders of the early church.

One of the worst things that happened to the Bible in the past two thousand years occurred in two stages—first in 1227, when University of Paris professor Stephen Langston divided the New Testament into chapters; the second in 1551, when a printer named Robert Stephanus, allegedly while riding on horseback from Lyons to Paris, numbered the sentences within Langston's chapters. Yes, chapters and verses are useful for references purposes—I've used them extensively here—but perhaps the damage chapters and verses cause outweighs such advantages. Since that time, Christians have come increasingly to view the Bible as a collection of isolated sentences pregnant with meaning in isolation from both their immediate and broader context.

Of course there can be meaning in individual Bible verses, but proof texting usually involves a presupposed position. The defender of this position then uses a concordance (or Bible software) to look up an associated keyword until he finds a verse that seems to support his position. If the verse is close, maybe he'll even look it up in various versions of the Bible to find the one that most clearly supports his position.

📖 Read Luke 14:26.

Describe how a cult leader might use this verse in trying to recruit a young person to his or her group.

_____

_____

_____

Reading Luke 14:26 out of context, without understanding the concept of ancient polemics, and ignoring the broader themes of the Bible opens up all sorts of abuses.

Did You Know?

MURATORIAN FRAGMENT

In 1740, Lodovico Muratori discovered an ancient document containing a list of writings used by the early church. Dating to about AD 180, the Muratorian Fragment, as it became known, is damaged, but it begins with Luke (cited as the third book of the Gospel) and includes every New Testament book except James, Hebrews, 3 John, 1 and 2 Peter, attesting to the very early acceptance of most of what became the canon. The document also lists the *Apocalypse of Peter* and the *Book of Wisdom* as authoritative books.

Sometimes people have the best of intentions in their proof texts. In *The Purpose Driven Life*, a runaway best seller that has undoubtedly helped many people come closer to God, Rick Warren quotes Psalm 2:4 ("*He who sits in the heavens laughs*") and suggests that his readers learn to laugh to be "more like God."

📖 Read Psalm 2:1–6.

Does the broader context of the first half of verse 4 support Warren's prescription?

_____

_____

_____

My purpose here is not to criticize Rick Warren, nor to minimize the value in much of what he wrote in *The Purpose Driven Life*, but rather to demonstrate how Scripture can be misused—even for good purposes—when we lift isolated verses.

One more example before we return to Philemon.

📖 Read 1 Peter 3:3–4.

How could someone misuse this passage?

_____

_____

_____

WHAT'S WRONG WITH BRAIDED HAIR?

Nothing! This is an example of a passage that is incomprehensible without cultural context. There are contemporary accounts of faddish, wealthy women braiding their hair into high piles with strings of jewels with the obvious intent to call attention to themselves. This is what Peter (and Paul in 1 Timothy 2:9) prohibits. Both apostles advise women to avoid such ostentatious shows. Dress modestly, both say, so the inner beauty of the Christian woman outshines any external display.

Taken to an extreme, an unscrupulous teacher might use this passage to insist Christian women should be naked! I suspect someone along the way has done precisely that, despite the obvious silliness.

What has all this have to do with Philemon? Prior to the Civil War in this country, much of the church used the Bible to defend slavery. I suspect much of the biblical proof texts used came from the Old Testament, but several came from the New Testament.

📖 Read Ephesians 6:5–9; 1 Corinthians 7:21.

Do these passages seem to support the institution of slavery?

_____

_____

_____

Paul was concerned with people's spiritual condition far more than their physical condition. Slavery was a fact of life in the Roman Empire—an institution that had become essential to cultural stability. Paul neither approves of nor condemns slavery anywhere. To him, enslavement to sin was a more significant issue than enslavement to a human, and freedom came only through faith in God. To suggest that Paul's advice to slaves (and their masters) endorses slavery is to ignore the totality of his message and the gospel. Yet that is what many American preachers did prior to the Civil War. Consider these examples:

"There is not one verse in the Bible inhibiting slavery, but many regulating it. It is not then, we conclude, immoral."— Alexander Campbell "The right of holding slaves is clearly established in the Holy Scriptures, both by precept and example."—Rev. R. Furman

"The doom of Ham has been branded on the form and features of his African descendants. The hand of fate has united his color and destiny. Man cannot separate what God hath joined."—U.S. Senator James Hammond

This kind of perverse thinking led the African-American abolitionist, orator, and statesman Frederick Douglass to respond vehemently. In an 1852 speech before the Ladies' Anti-Slavery Society of Rochester, New York, Douglass said, "For my part, I would say, welcome infidelity! welcome atheism! welcome anything! in preference to the gospel, as preached by those Divines [preachers]. They convert the very name of religion into an engine of tyranny, and barbarous cruelty, and serve to confirm more infidels, in this age, than all the infidel writings. . . . These ministers make religion a cold and flinty-hearted thing, having neither principles of right action, nor bowels of compassion."

What primarily separated Douglass from the religious slavery supporters lay in his use of Scripture as a whole rather than a collection of proof texts. In the speech, he made no attempt to out-proof-text his opponents. Instead, he rightly understood the gospel holistically as a message of love, compassion, brotherhood, and freedom.

📖 Read Philemon 8–21.

What is Paul's primary purpose in writing to Philemon?

_____

_____

_____

Proslavery forces used Philemon to argue it was a Christian's responsibility to return escaped slaves. Do you see this as a valid use of Philemon?

_____

_____

_____

The proslavery argument must have gone something like this: Onesimus was an escaped slave belonging to Philemon; Paul came into contact with Onesimus; Paul returned Onesimus to Philemon; therefore, Paul teaches Christians should return escaped slaves to their owners.

But the argument ignores two critical elements of Paul's letter. What are they?

_____

_____

_____

First of all, Paul never acknowledges any responsibility to return Onesimus to Philemon. He sends Onesimus back because he *preferred to do nothing without [Philemon's] consent* (v. 14). Most important, Paul asks Philemon to receive Onesimus *"no longer as a slave"* (v. 16). Displaying loving tact, Paul

Frederick Douglass, who wrote, "This existence of slavery in this country brands . . . your Christianity as a lie."

"So if you consider me your partner, receive him as you would receive me."

Philemon 17

asks Philemon to free Onesimus because of the brotherhood they share as disciples of Christ Jesus.

We have no record of Philemon's response, but it is almost impossible to believe he could fail to respond to Paul's request.

LEARNING FROM PHILEMON

APPLY On Day One of this study, we looked at the problem of wealth and the responsibilities of the wealthy. Are you wealthy?

_____

_____

_____

If you're an American, your answer probably should be yes. By world standards, even the poorest Americans are relatively wealthy.

APPLY Regardless of your income, how can you use your relative wealth in ways that enhance the teaching of the gospel in your area?

_____

_____

_____

For my own part, I recognize I stand condemned by my own question. I do not always use my wealth in ways consistent with my beliefs. As one small effort along those lines, I ask my publisher, AMG, to forward any royalties beyond the advance to World Vision to help in its attempt to ease the suffering of children across the globe.

On Days Two and Three, we looked at Paul's strategies in spreading the gospel. Do you think strategies and tactics are important in Christian efforts to preach the Word? Why or why not?

_____

_____

_____

_____

_____

We Americans are part of many different Christian traditions (unfortunately so in some ways). Does your church have strategies to advance the gospel? If so, how can you help advance them? If not, how can you help your church develop some?

_____

_____

_____

Do you think Paul's strategies have twenty-first century corollaries? If so, how might they be applied?

_____

_____

_____

_____

On Day Four, we looked at how Philemon and other biblical passages were used to justify slavery in the United States. Slavery has long since been abolished in this country, but oppression has not disappeared.

What are some examples of modern-day oppression, and what responsibility do the church and individual Christians have to oppose these practices?

_____

_____

_____

_____

While I know there are political arguments about the topic, one example I might offer is the treatment of illegal or undocumented aliens in this country. What lesson does Paul's letter to Philemon provide on this issue?

_____

_____

_____

_____

In contradiction to any Bible-based support of slavery and other forms of oppression, Paul wrote, "_There is neither Jew nor Greek, there is neither slave nor free, there is neither male nor female, for you are all one in Christ Jesus_" (Galatians 3:28).

APPLY How does this principle apply to our relationships with others?

_____

_____

_____

_____

Do you treat others as if you are one with them in Christ Jesus? If not, what specific things can you do to correct this?

_____

_____

_____

_____

_____

_____